CLASSIC American RACING MOTORCYCLES

MARK
87

CLASSIC American RACING MOTORCYCLES

Mick Walker

Page 1
Lance Weil brought this special 883cc XLR-TT racer over to Britain in 1967. He is pictured here in winning form at Lydden Hill, 2 July that year

Page 2
1972 AMA Champion Mark Brelsford power slides the XR750 to yet another ½-mile oval victory

Right
Edwin Burgess (1250 cc Indian) winning the open class at Ascarate Speedway in the period immediately following the Second World War

Published in 1992 by Osprey Publishing
59 Grosvenor Street, London W1X 9DA

Cataloguing in Publication Data is available from the British Library

ISBN 1-85532-233-1

Editor Shaun Barrington
Page design Geoffrey Wadsley

Filmset in Great Britain by
Tradespools Ltd, Frome, Somerset
Printed by BAS Printers Limited,
Over Wallop, Hampshire

ARATE SPEEDWAY
Have a Coke

Harley-Davidson star Cal Rayborn leads Ray Pickrell in the Anglo-American Match Races, Mallory Park, 2 April 1972. He won the race

Contents

	About the author	8
	Introduction	9
1	Early days	14
2	Daytona Beach	29
3	Catalina Island	44
4	The Harley saga	50
5	Desert racing	76
6	Dirt track	81
7	AMA	94
8	Bonneville Salt Flats	107
9	Daytona International Speedway	117
10	Transatlantic	146
11	King Kenny	160
12	Latin brothers – South America	172
	Index	190

About the author

Mick Walker is an enthusiast for all forms of motorcycle sport. He has been a successful competitor and has helped many to triumph with his profound knowledge of tuning. There is virtually no aspect of the business in which Mick has not been active at some point, and that includes being an importer of exotic Italian race-bred machines. Today, he heads a thriving company that specializes in the supply of spare parts to Ducati owners and racers around the world. He is also one of Osprey's most prolific authors.

Mick rode a variety of racers during the classic era, including an AJS 7R, Manx Norton, Greeves Silverstone, a brace of BSA Gold Stars, various Ducatis and even 50 and 125 cc Hondas.

Above
The author raced a wide range of machinery over almost a decade, encompassing most of the 1960s. He finally hung up his leathers in 1972.

Introduction

In this, the fifth of the *Classic Racing Motorcycles* series, it is America's turn to come under the spotlight.

Motorcycle racing in the USA was in a time warp for many years – thanks in no small part to the rules and regulations adopted by the sport's organising body in that vast country, the AMA (American Motorcycle Association) which was formed in the 1920s. From then until the late 1960s Stateside racing went its own way, bringing with it decades of voluntary isolation. However, before and after, the United States was to occupy an outstanding place in world motorcycling history.

First, at the turn of the century came the large capacity machines from the likes of Indian, Excelsior and Harley-Davidson which not only dominated at home, but abroad too. Indian, Excelsior and Harley-Davidson established themselves with thundering v-twins, while ACE and Henderson followed the lead of automobile manufacturers and built motorcycles with large capacity four cylinder engines. Curtiss went one better and built a *V-8*, as early as 1907! By 1913 American companies had attained an annual production output of some 70,000 machines, a considerable number of which were destined for the European market.

This situation was to change drastically after the

Dirt track, a thrilling feature of Stateside motorcycle racing for many years

The

32
TRIUMPH

Left
Joe Leonard streaking past the flagman to win the 1958 Daytona 200 miles over the old beach circuit

Below left
Ron Grant (with cap) raced this works 500 Triumph in the one and only Canadian World Championship GP at Mosport in 1967. Rod Coates, Triumph's American Competition boss is on the left

Great War, when Henry Ford's Model T turned America's attention away from two wheels to four. The Europeans, led by Britain, now took over motorcycle sport and during the 1920s and 1930s were in the ascendancy. Meanwhile Stateside bike builders either went to the wall, or at best simply got by with reduced production levels for local markets, and American motorcycle racing evolved along totally different lines from European racing.

Essentially the difference centred around outright capacity and speed in the States, whilst in Europe handling and braking were equally important values, not just maximum power figures. Poor sales also played their part, and by the end of the Second World War the United States had only two major manufacturers left, Harley-Davidson and Indian; and by 1953 Indian themselves were on the rocks.

Thereafter Harley-Davidson quietly dominated on both road and track, until first the British and later the Japanese staged a virtual take over of the giant American market. This commercial success also led to these two countries making in-roads into American racing. However, this was partly thwarted by the AMA who used their rule book to 'protect'

Pat Hennen (in Bell Tee-shirt) and brother Chuck in their 'camp' at the 1976 Dutch TT. Pat was one of the first American stars to make it in Europe before a serious accident in the 1978 Isle of Man Senior TT ended his racing career

Japanese machines began to make a significant impact on American racing during the late 1960s. Photo shows Yamaha rider Art Baumann in the summer of 1969

Harley-Davidson until the passing of the 'Formula 750' rule in late 1969. Thereafter the floodgates were opened and American road racing was never to be the same again. But if Harley-Davidson could no longer be assured of victory, this move did bring American riders out of isolation and onto the world stage. By the late 1970s men like Kenny Roberts, Steve Baker, Pat Hennen and Randy Mamola were household names on both sides of the Atlantic. The 1980s saw this trend continue until a point has been reached in the 1990s where an American is expected to win the 500 cc World Championship, the blue riband of motorcycle sport.

Because of this evolution process it has not been possible to write a book covering simply American bikes; other countries having provided the main platforms upon which American riders have taken over the world. So *Classic American Racing Motorcycles* is about the men and events which shaped history, rather than the motorcycles – many of which were not of Amerian manufacture. The final chapter covers South American racing history. In many ways of vital importance to the overall picture, these Latin cousins were often the trendsetters, with their Northern cousins following at a later date. The American racing story is a unique one filled with interest and drama throughout, making this a particularly fascinating title to compile.

Many good people have helped towards the completion of *Classic Amerian Racing Motorcycles* in some way. As I have discovered in the past, the vast majority were only too pleased to provide whatever assistance they could, and I will always be in their debt. Unfortunately, the list is almost endless, so I must apologise to those whose names I have not been able to include, but I shall be eternally grateful to them for the help given.

So I offer acknowledgment to the following in no particular order of merit: Doug Jackson, Brian Woolley, Philip Tooth, Barry Hickmott, Don Mitchell, John Fernley, Nick Nicholls, Peter Hageman, Peter Brushwood, Michael Dregni, Barry Sheene, Ron Grant and the staff of the Daytona International Speedway.

The photographs came from a number of sources including Doug Jackson's World Motorcycle News Agency, Harley-Davidson, Zanella, Nick Nicholls, Richard Walker, the EMAP Archives and my own collection. I have used as many previously unpublished photographs as I could, but occasionally it has been necessary to use a 'familiar' picture due to its historic significance. As usual the excellent cover photography is the work of Don Morley.

I would also record the patience shown by my dear wife Susan, and the efforts of Kim White, who typed the manuscript. Last, but not least, the super efficient Osprey editorial team under editor Shaun Barrington, not forgetting the encouragement provided by Osprey's editorial manager, Nicholas Collins.

Classic American Racing Motorcycles continues the review of countries that manufactured and raced motorcycles during the 'classic' period, begun with the British title and continued by the Japanese, German and Italian volumes. I hope that you will garner as much pleasure from reading the finished work as I have had in compiling it.

Mick Walker
Wisbech, Cambridgeshire

1
Early Days

The United States can rightly be regarded as one of the true pioneering countries in the birth of the motorcycle – both for street and competition use. During the first decade of the Twentieth Century the American industry grew at a tremendous rate, with the likes of Excelsior, Harley-Davidson, Indian and Flying Merkel leading the way. In fact by the year 1911 there were over 100 makes of motorcycle being produced in the USA. However, much of this early effort was very much of the 'boom and bust' variety and by 1913 the figure was down to 40 – and by 1920 only a handful remained.

From a racing viewpoint the first manufacturers to enter the ring were Indian and Curtiss. The former concern was the result of two former racing cyclists, George M Hendee and Carl Oscar Hedstrom pooling their resources in 1901, to form the fledgling Hendee Manufacturing Company which that year produced a grand total of *three* motorcycles under the Indian banner. The pair had first met the previous year when Hedstrom was demonstrating a motor powered pacing bicycle of his own design and manufacture.

The first Indian motorcycles to take part in a competition event appeared in July 1902 when three examples were entered in the Boston–New York endurance run – the first such event ever staged in the States. In true pioneering fashion Hendee and Hedstrom acted as riders, together with George N Holden. The trio scored a resounding 1, 2, 3 to firmly establish the Indian name in the record books. On 5 September 1903 Indian rider Holden won the country's first long distance track race at the Brighton Beach dirt track, New York City.

These early Indian machines employed a single cylinder 'bought-in' engine produced for them by the Thor Manufacturing Co. Another feature of the Indian marque from its earliest days was chain final drive (most competitors at that time employed belts).

The first of the famous v-twins did not appear until 1905, George Holden again grabbed the headlines when he and Louis Mueller established a new coast-to-coast record of 31 days, 12 hours and 15 minutes. But in terms of importance to the company's affairs this achievement was overshadowed by the fact that Indian were in future to build their own engines, together with Hedstrom carburettors, and to this end new, larger production facilities had been erected on State Street, Springfield, Massachusetts. That same year Jake De Rosier rode one of the prototype v-twins in several races.

One of the first fruits of the move to larger premises was the announcement, for 1907, of the first production Indian v-twin. The angle between the cylinders was extremely narrow – only 42 degrees – and the rear cylinder, as on the single, served as a seat tube.

One of the twins, a 37-inch (600 cc) model was sent to Britain, where the American rider T K Hastings rode it in the 1907 Thousand Mile Trial organised by the ACC (Auto Cycle Club) – itself a forerunner of the ACU (Auto Cycle Union). This event was later to evolve into the famous ISDT (International Six Days Trial). It was the first time that an American machine ridden by an American had won a British motorcycle competiton event. By 1908 speed contests had largely replaced endurance runs and it was in the former arena that De Rosier became an official (paid!) Indian rider.

1908 also saw the launch of the Springfield company's first production model intended solely as a racing job. Equipped with a diamond frame, the 'over-the-counter' Indian racer could be supplied in both single or twin cylinder variants. The twin was 61 inch (1,000 cc), the single 30.5 inch (500 cc); valve gear was ioe (inlet over exhaust). 'Swede' Swenson won the 978 mile New York–Chicago race in 33 hours, 26 minutes; while in Britain T K Hastings repeated his victory of 12 months earlier by winning the 1908 Thousand Mile Trial.

An early Harley-Davidson competitor. Together with Indian and Curtiss the Milwaukee company was among the pioneers of the American motorcycle on both street and track. This example was used for both racing and hill climbing

The other famous American *racing* marque of that first decade of the Twentieth Century was Curtiss. The man behind these unique bikes was none other than Glenn H Curtiss, far better known today for his aviation, rather than motorcycling expertise. But in those veteran and vintage days Mr Curtiss was to play a prominent role in the birth of the racing motorcycle in the USA.

A Curtiss first came to the fore in the Autumn of 1902, when an example made the fastest time for a 'standard machine' in the New York Motorcycle Club's road race. The following Spring (May 1903) Glenn Curtiss himself became the first man to win an American hill climb. Shortly afterwards Curtiss set a new one-mile speed record at an average speed of 63.8 mph on a 680 cc single cylinder machine of his own design. Further speed events followed including a 10 mile sprint along the shores of Ormond Beach (right next to Daytona!), Florida on 28 January 1904, where Glenn Curtiss averaged 67.3 mph. This was to remain undefeated for the next four years.

In early 1904 the Curtiss twin became the first motorcycle in history with twistgrip controls (not rivals Indian who publicly claimed that they were the first). The Curtiss plant was at Hammondsport, New York; but it was again at Ormond Beach, Florida that Glenn Curtiss' finest motorcycling hour was to take place. This came on 28 January 1907 when the great rider/engineer earned the title of the 'fastest man in the world' when he rode a 40 bhp *V-8* of his own design at 136.3 mph – a faster speed than had ever been made by any type of vehicle. Unfortunately this was never officially sanctioned, as later during the 'official' run the universal joint disintegrated, to be followed by a buckled frame; causing the speed test to be abandoned. The V-8's *claimed* 136 mph plus was not to be officially exceeded until almost a quarter of a century later in 1930!

Glenn Curtiss also constructed a three-cylinder 1,500 cc model with a claimed maximum speed of 90 mph; but by 1909 his interest in two-wheelers was beginning to wane, replaced instead by a burning desire to become an aircraft builder – a dream which he was to realise and in the process Glenn H Curtiss became one of his country's greatest aviators.

Meanwhile Indian had established a London office

with rider Billy Wells in charge. And it was Wells who persuaded Hendee and Hedstrom to have a major stab at the Isle of Man TT races which had begun in 1907. To this effect Indian produced a number of specially prepared v-twins with the engine capacity reduced to 750 cc. For the 1909 races Billy Wells included himself in a trio of riders (the others were Gordon Fletcher and Guy Lee Evans); however Wells was sidelined from the proceedings due to a practice crash. At that time the rules allowed either 500 cc singles or 750 cc twins, the latter in view of the poor showing by the twins in earlier years. The 1908 winner Jack Marshall (Triumph single) was first away but was soon caught by Lee Evans and Harry Collier (Matchless twin). Although Marshall fought back, the final result after 10 laps (158 miles) was: Collier, Lee Evans and Marshall.

Left
Hillclimbing was an important facet of early American motorcycle sport. Here a rider begins to lose traction on the final section and tries to 'Walk it out' in an effort to help his spinning rear wheel from digging in

Below
Hillclimbing attracted many spectators. They usually watched from their parked cars. Whenever a rider went over the top, every car's horn blew in acclaim

This produced a lot of publicity for Indian on both sides of the Atlantic and the result was another Indian 'invasion' in 1910 – the last meeting to be staged over the original short St John's course. In addition the twins' maximum capacity was reduced from 750 cc to 670 cc for the race. This time there were four private Indian entries (amongst them W O Bentley, later to win fame and fortune as a manufacturer of prestige motor cars) in addition to the official works team. But Lady Luck was against the 'Iron Redskins' that year, with only two privateers surviving: Scotsman Jimmy Alexander in 14th and Arthur Moorhouse 21st places.

But the moment of Manx glory which the Springfield company had tried to achieve eventually came at the third attempt. The 1911 TT headlines read: 'A clean sweep for Indian'. And this came even though the capacity ceiling for the twin cylinder model had again been reduced, this time to 585 cc. The 1911 Senior TT was run without the British Rudge team who had withdrawn as a result of their young rider, Vic Surridge, becoming the first TT fatality after crashing in practice. It was also the first year of the now legendary $37\frac{3}{4}$-mile Snaefell Mountain Circuit.

All eyes were on the Matchless twin and the bright scarlet Indians, one of which was to be ridden by the flamboyant American, Jake De Rosier. In fact, it was De Rosier who gained a full half-minute lead over the Matchless star Charlie Collier, only to crash

Indian rider Bill Tuman after taking victory in the 20-mile National at Bay Meadows, 22 June 1952. Tuman set up a new US record for the distance, winning in 14 minutes, 41.9 seconds

on the approach to Ramsey, bending his machine in the process – he eventually remounted and struggled on to finish 12th.

Collier was forced to stop to take on fuel out on the course but kept in front of Oliver Godfrey on another Indian. Another fuel stop for Collier let Godfrey into the lead and he went on to score the first ever 'foreign' victory in the TT series for the Indian factory. When it was revealed that Collier had been disqualified for taking on petrol away from the official refuelling depot the Americans were able to rejoice in a hat-trick with Franklin second and Moorhouse third!

During 1910, Oscar Hedstrom had begun mapping out new four and eight valve singles and v-twins and, from the middle of 1911 (but after the Isle of Man victory), these appeared and were to form the mainspring of Indian's racing and record attempts until the mid 1920s. It is interesting to realise that the four valve per cylinder layout was not intended as a means of extra power, but to improve reliability; it was none the less a noteworthy technical achievement.

Besides the 1911 success, Indian's most famous overseas performance was at the Brooklands circuit in England, where C B Franklin rode one of the new eight valve Indians to cover 300 miles in less than

300 minutes (4 hours, 42 minutes to be exact), establishing official world speed records for the 2, 4, 5, and 6 hour periods.

Back in America board tracks (otherwise known as motordromes) had arrived in 1908 and quickly spread to dominate motorcycle sport across the States for the next few years. Essentially this form of racing took place over a short ($\frac{1}{3}$ or $\frac{1}{4}$ mile) wooden oval, with the corners banked at an angle of 25 degrees (later increased until 60 degrees was standard). De Rosier and Indian soon became the star combination at these events. His riding ability on these tiny ovals was awesome, and his fame spread like wildfire.

So what of that famous American two wheeled institution, Harley-Davidson? Well, Harley-Davidson were to prove a slow starter in the racing game. Formed in 1903 it was to be 10 years and 1913 before the Milwaukee company dipped its toe into the white hot cauldron of motorcycle sport. This was quite strange because from that time onwards the name Harley-Davidson was to loom large in the sphere of American bike racing.

The first Harleys to take part were very much private entries; however, it was not long before the factory threw its full weight into committing pukka works machinery to the task of *winning* . . . Harley-Davidson wasn't interested in coming second. For a start it not only signed up Bill Ottaway from the Thor concern, where he had been the engineering backroom wizard behind Thor's racing involvement for some years, but also the Harley management realised that if it was to go racing then the proper financial commitment would have to be made. This professional attitude was to be the hallmark of the Milwaukee concern throughout the forthcoming decades . . . and maybe this is the *real* key to why in the 1990s Harley-Davidson are the USA's sole surviving player on the world motorcycle stage.

Harley's inaugural race came on 4 July 1914, at the Dodge City, Kansas 300 mile road race. It wasn't to prove a fairy tale debut as the race was won by an Indian, with only two Harleys surviving the distance, and then well down the field. But at least it was a start. By 1915 Harley-Davidson was closely challenging Indian for the number one spot in American racing, with the likes of Cyclone, Emblem, Excelsior, Flying Merkel and Pope giving chase. A year later, 1916, Bill Harley and his engineering right hand man Bill Ottaway at last finished their own eight valve v-twin to challenge the might of Indian who had had their own eight valver for the previous five years.

Indian responded by coming out with the new

John Wood speeding round the Laconia, New Hampshire circuit on his Harley-Davidson V-twin, June 1953

Brad Andres (11) winner of the 1955 National Championship at Dodge City battles with fellow Harley rider, John Gibson

side-valve Powerplus engine designed by Charles Gustafson, who had replaced Oscar Hedstrom after the latter had left Indian following a disagreement with co-founder George Hendee. These early Stateside racing days were nothing if not political . . . not only this but Indian's star rider Jake De Rosier had been fired by Hendee at the end of 1911. He subsequently rode for the Excelsior factory, but was never to achieve the successes he had gained on the 'Iron Redskin', dying in 1913 following an operation on a badly damaged leg sustained in a racing accident the previous year. De Rosier could rightly be proclaimed as America's original motorcycle racing super star, with some 1,000 competitive events spanning the years 1898–1912.

The other rider of note to straddle an Excelsior in those early days was Lee Humiston, who in 1912 secured himself a lasting place in the history of motorcycling by becoming the first man in the world to *officially* exceed 100 mph on two wheels (Curtiss' 1907 figure was unsanctioned). However the Excelsior rider's speed was only recognised by the FAM (Federation of American Motorcyclists).

The United States' entry into the Great War saw motorcycle competition come to a virtual halt in 1917 and 1918; this was as much due to a mutual

agreement to cease participation by Excelsior, Harley-Davidson and Indian, as to the outbreak of war itself. Both Harley-Davidson and Indian were to supply many thousands of machines to the American government for the Allied war effort, adding millions of dollars to their respective turnovers.

When peace finally came at the end of 1918 the Stateside based motorcycle manufacturers found that they had a new enemy, the affordable motor car, in the shape of Henry Ford's Model T. Although it had first made its debut back in October 1907, it was not until 1915 when the price had dropped by *half* and production vastly increased, that the Model T first posed a serious challenge to motorcycle sales. But in the immediate aftermath of the war and throughout the 1920s this problem accelerated as more and more Americans bought four wheels instead of two. This in turn meant that two-wheel manufacturers had less and less money with which to go racing.

To start with the likes of Excelsior, Harley-Davidson and Indian put on a brave face and still continued to pour large sums of money into ever more competitive speed machines. It is interesting to note that the first two *officially* FIM recognised world speed records after the First World War went to American motorcycles.

First there was Eugene 'Gene' Walker who clocked 103.5 mph on his works supported 994 cc Indian v-twin at Daytona Beach on 14 April 1920; followed by Britain's Freddie Dixon who broke this figure with a speed of 106.5 mph on one of the 989 cc v-twin Harley-Davidsons at Arpajon, France on 9 September 1923. Very shortly afterwards Dixon and Harley-Davidson lost the record to Temple and British Anzani; an American machine not holding

Brad Andres (centre) smiles broadly after winning the 1955 Daytona 200 mile race; his father Leonard is on the rider's left

Below
A group of riders at the Laconia 100-mile championship meeting, June 1958. Note typical period Stateside riding gear, complete with 'Space' helmets and lace-up boots

Right
Laconia race paddock, June 1959. Evident is the great mixture of machinery including domestic Harleys, British Triumphs and BSAs, and German Zündapps

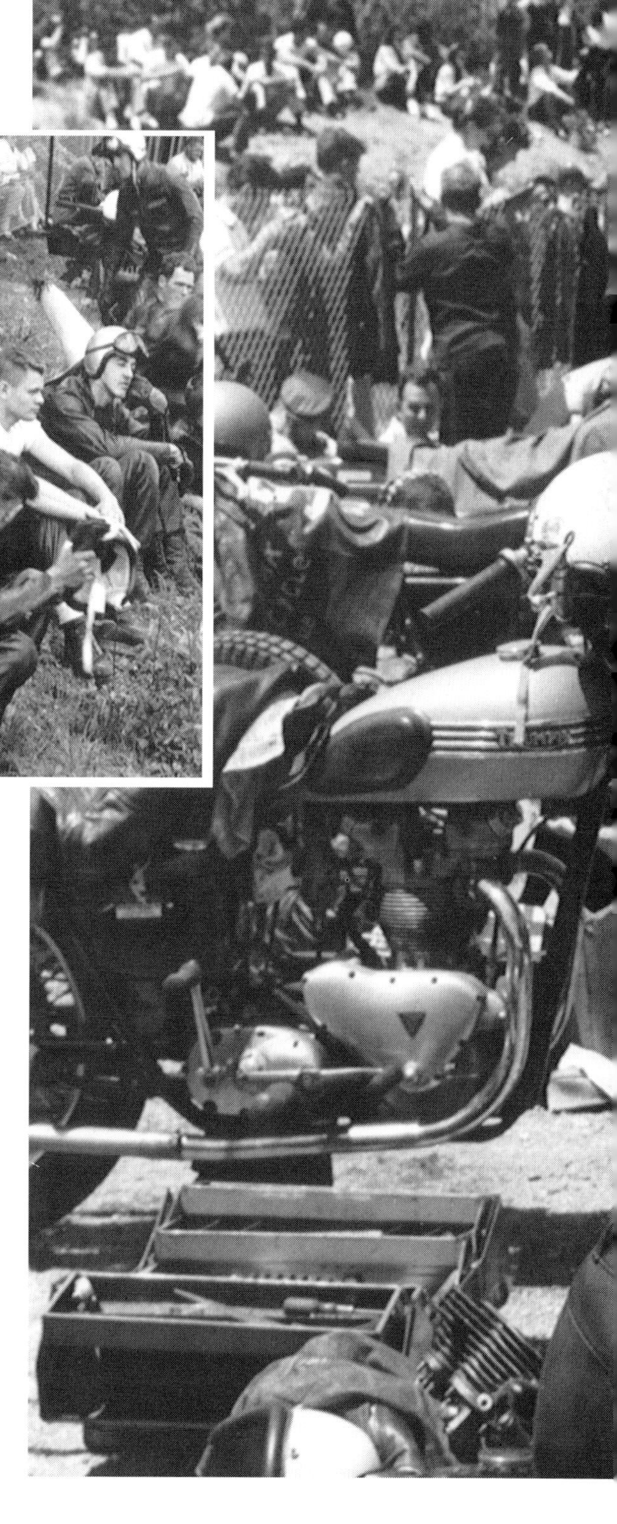

the 'World's Fastest' again until Cal Rayborn and Harley-Davidson reclaimed it for the Stars and Stripes in October 1970 (see Chapter 8).

As for pukka racing events, the pre-war Motordromes had not survived – thanks in no small part to their poor safety record, with both riders and spectators suffering fatalities. In their place came a combination of dirt racing over existing horse tracks (see Chapter 6) and Board-track automobile speedway. The latter venues were ovals varying in length from one mile to two and a half miles. The board surfaces were constructed like the earlier, defunct motordromes, but the big auto speedways were considerably larger (and vastly safer!) than the much shorter pre-war motorcycle-only saucers. Though the banking didn't generally tilt as steeply as in the old 'dromes, the racing speeds were truly sensational for the period. For example, the board speedway at Altoona, Pennsylvania, was a mile and a quarter around, and the promoters enthused over its 120 mph lap potential.

157

And it was at Altoona that the name of Joe Petrali (Excelsior) burst onto the national scene, when in 1925 he won the 100-mile AMA National Championship averaging 100.32 mph. Earlier the same day, Harley-Davidson works rider Jim Davis had won the five mile event at a blistering 110.7 mph (to put these times into perspective, Peter De Paolo won the 1925 Indianapolis 500 automobile race at 101.13 mph).

A major problem with the board speedway tracks was that they needed massive crowds to survive; part of this was because as the speedways aged, maintenance costs shot up. Entire sections of boarding had to be replaced. Unlike tarmac or concrete, wood rotted and riders couldn't race on shaky, splintery surfaces. In addition as urban populations grew, the speedways found themselves surrounded by neighbours who didn't want noise on their doorsteps. The final nail in the coffin for board speedway was the Great Depression which came in late 1929 and lasted until well into the new decade. Strangely perhaps, that very special form of American motorcycle racing – dirt track (otherwise known as flat-track) – not only survived but prospered during the late 1920s and throughout the 1930s.

Another important segment of Stateside sport during this period was hill climbing. Although there were hill climbers who rode professionally (Joe Petrali for Excelsior and then Harley-Davidson, Orie Steele for Indian) the vast majority of hill climb bikes were near standard models modified by their owners. In this sport the true amateur could race what he owned, since there were classes for almost every size of production-based machine. Compared to any other kind of pukka competition, hill climbing was an inexpensive, low-pressure sport.

By the mid 1920s the major manufacturers and the AMA (American Motorcycle Association), the new motorcycle sporting organisation in the United States, decided that racing had to be less specialised *and* less costly (actually the two went together). It was decreed that the exotic works machines had to be abandoned. This entailed a change of rules (catalogued in Chapter 7) to allow amateurs more chance of success – and so the AMA established *Class C* racing (A and B were the old categories for special one-off works racing machines). Class C was a road-going based formula, in other words the bikes had to be stock designs – as manufactured and sold. Class C did not become fully effective until the mid 1930s.

Of all the standard machines in the USA during

Laconia came closer than most American events to European racing during the 1950s. But the riders still dragged their feet through the turns!

Top three at Laconia 1960. Left to right: Carroll Resweber (Harley-Davidson), Dick Mann (BSA) and Roger Reiman (Harley-Davidson)

the 1930s the most obvious machines to come within the Class C rule book were the 45-inch (750 cc) v-twins – Harley-Davidson's model W and Indian's Scout. The machines were somewhat lighter (but still overweight by prevailing European standards) than the larger capacity American monsters, but sufficiently powerful to make racing them interesting.

But Class C racing didn't entirely kill the factory teams; what it did do was to create a 'jack of all trades' the same riders competing in dirt track racing, hill climbing, record breaking – you name it, the 1930s American competition rider was expected to do it all. Leading all these was Harley-Davidson's star of the 1930s, Joe Petrali. Unfortunately as the years passed he would become the forgotten man of Stateside motorcycle racing. Petrali reached the pinnacle of his career in 1935 when he won countless races including every Class A National Championship race. He was also the top hill climber in each category that year.

Just about the biggest real race of the era was the

ARLE
AVIDSO
1
1

AMA National 200 mile Championship. This was held at Savannah, Georgia until it was transferred to Daytona Beach in 1937 (see Chapter 2).

By the late 1930s Harley-Davidson and Indian were the two dominant marques. In January 1936 Indian mounted Ed Kretz had won the 200-mile Class C National Championship at Savannah at an average speed of 70.03 mph. This was the beginning of a four-year period when the Springfield, Massachusetts concern, helped in no small way by the riding talents of Ed Kretz, was the team to beat.

From 1937 through to 1941 Kretz ran up a truly impressive race record. He not only won the inaugural Daytona 200 on the beach in January 1937, but also led each of the successive four pre-war 200-milers before being forced to retire. He won two consecutive 100-mile Nationals at the legendary Langhorne, Pennsylvania, one-mile dirt oval in 1937 and 1938, and he won again in 1940. In 1938 Kretz took the very first Laconia National, a 200-mile event which came nearest to a European type road race at the time. This event was so hectic and demanding that it earned Kretz the nickname 'Iron Man' which was to stick with him for the remainder of his career.

The year 1939 was significant in the American racing story, if not directly to do with American-made machines. This heralded the first major C Class victory by a foreign motorcycle, when Robert Sparks won the Langhorne 100 on an ohc Norton.

The next major step in the evolution of American racing came in 1941 – on the very eve of the country's entry into the Second World War. This was the arrival on the scene of the Harley-Davidson WR, the mainstay of Harley-Davidson racing for the next eight racing seasons (in other words 1941, 1946–1952). It was also the forerunner of the even more famous and influential motorcycle, the K series, which went on to dominate racing the length and breadth of the USA for an amazing seventeen years spanning the period 1953–1969. Never again would Indian dominate as it had in the period up to the outbreak of the Second World War. In the place of the furious Harley v Indian duels there was to emerge an even greater battle between first the British and ultimately the Japanese for supremacy in the American motorcycle racing scene. The 'classic' era was about to begin.

Left
Winner of the coveted AMA Number 1 plate for 1960, Harley-Davidson's Carroll Resweber

Below
Resweber gunning his 750 KR side valve Harley to yet another victory in the summer of 1960

A leading contender for Stateside racing honours during the late 1950s and early 1960s, the 499 cc BSA Gold Star. American tuners could extract well over 50 bhp from this British single cylinder pushrod engine

2

Daytona Beach

Anyone who thinks that Daytona is a relative newcomer to the world of motor sport is in for a real surprise, because in fact its story starts way back at the beginning of the Twentieth Century.

At that time the sprawling Ormond Hotel was a popular haunt for wealthy American industrialists who travelled south by the railroad system to take full advantage of the clear blue skies of Florida. Amongst these 'Captains of Industry' was Ransom Olds, founder of Oldsmobile and his friend Alexander Winton, another of the American pioneer auto manufacturers. And it was not long before both were sampling the delights of speeding up and down the gleaming silver sands of the Ormond and Daytona beaches.

Legend has it that both clocked almost 60 mph during a highly unofficial burn-up in 1902. This event caused quite a sensation – and perhaps more importantly reminded the Ormond Hotel proprietors of a proposal they had received some four years earlier in 1898 from a cycling journalist, William Morgan. Morgan had broached the idea of staging a cycle week on the beach, with the Ormond as its headquarters. With the advent of the motor car, they saw this as a way of attracting wealthier visitors to their hotel. Subsequently, Morgan, who by then was working for a car journal, was invited down to Florida to map out details of Daytona's first organised speed event, actually called the Ormond Beach

The famous Daytona beach and road circuit as it was in the late 1940s

Robert Cartwright (98) powers his Harley-Davidson V-twin around one of the turns during the 1949 100-mile Amateur Race

Racing Tournament, which took place in February 1903. Morgan's magazine and the Ormond Hotel owners acted as joint sponsors for the new event, with Alexander Winton appropriately making the fastest time at 68.19 mph.

In 1905 the world's first car drag race took place on the beach. Previously competitors had run individually with the time keepers deciding the results. But, in 1905, a special event was held with a four car final won by Louis Ross driving a steam-powered Stanley. From a standing start, it beat the world's premier cars over the measured mile, including a Mercedes-Benz which had earlier established a world speed record of 109 mph on the beach. For this feat Louis was acclaimed as the 'Speed King of the World'.

Bikes had been in the frame the previous year, when Glenn Curtiss the famous aviation pioneer (see Chapter 1) became the first American to clock a mile a minute on two wheels. He used a twin cylinder engine of his own design, which later that year was used to power America's first airship, the *Californian Arrow*. As recorded in the previous chapter Curtiss went on to build a V-8 motorcycle which (although

never sanctioned) achieved over 136 mph on Ormond Beach in 1907.

During the 1920s and early 1930s the Florida beach was to witness a number of speed record attempts. Sir Henry Seagrave and Malcolm Campbell fought for the honour of being the world's fastest man on four wheels, when they aimed their British-built monster cars along Daytona's thin strip of silver sand.

The year 1935 saw Campbell, piloting his legendary car Bluebird, push the record up to 276 mph, and on one run achieve an amazing 330 mph! But those sorts of speeds were simply just too great for such a narrow course and Daytona's era as a land speed record centre was brought to a close. The departure of the record breakers had one advantage: it forced the local authorities to look around for another major attraction, and that brought about the use of the venue as a combined beach-road circuit where the famous Daytona 200 was to run from 1937 until 1960.

The original course south of the Daytona town was 3.2 miles long, with a flat-out blind down the beach, a 180-degree corner on sand, then full throttle again along a narrow, undulating tarmac road which ran parallel to the beach behind the sand dunes and back to the beach via another 180-degree turn.

The beach/road circuit was used for the first time (by cars) in 1936. Two wheelers made their debut in 1937; enthusiasts in the Southern States having staged a 200-mile race for the AMA championship – originally at Savannah, Georgia, then at Jacksonville in 1934 and 1935 before returning to Savannah in 1936. Thanks to some forward thinking by Daytona Beach officials, the organisers (the Southern Motorcycle Association) were persuaded to move the race again, this time to the Florida coast.

The first Daytona 200 took place on 24 January 1937 in front of some 15,000 spectators. From a field of 98 riders the winner was Ed Kretz who rode the same Indian side valve 42 degree v-twin Sport Scout that he had ridden to victory at Savannah the previous year. This machine ran on a compression ratio of 6.5:1 and breathed through a $1\frac{1}{2}$-inch (38 mm)

Another view of the 1949 Daytona Amateur Race, Pete Folse (35) from Tampa, Florida in the lead at the South Turn

Norton
14
14
Norton

AMOCO
15
122

Above left
British Manx Nortons dominated the 1949 200 mile Experts Race; the winner was 20-year old Dick Klamfoth from Groveport, Ohio

Above
Billy Mathews (98), winner of the 1950 200-miler, with runner-up Dick Klamfoth (2) and fourth-placeman Bill Tuman. All rode Norton singles. The legendary British tuner Francis Beart is second left, wearing sunglasses

Left
Daytona 1950; riders fuelling up prior to the race

Linkert carburettor. On 4.33 gearing the bike would run at 114 mph on the fastest sections of the Daytona beach/road course.

Second came Clark Turnbull on a Norton, whilst Harley-Davidson's Ellis Pearce was third. All three riders covered 63 laps. Kretz's winning average speed was 74.10 mph. As in subsequent years, all machines had to comply with the AMA's Class C rules.

In the next three seasons Indian's greatest rivals Harley-Davidson won the Daytona 200, under the riding of Benny Campanale (1938 and 1939) and Babe

Below
Third place in the 1951 100-mile Amateur Race went to the young Texan Al Gunter (later to become a famous Indianapolis Stock Car driver) who rode a BSA Gold Star. Standing with him left to right: Jack White KLG representative, George Britton BSA dealer from Dallas, Texas and Brian Martindale who managed Gunter's pit during the race

Above
Start of the 1950 200-mile Expert Race. This leading group of riders include Harley-Davidson, Indian and Norton machinery

Right
Practice for the 1952 100-mile Amateur race

Tancrede (1940). As a testament to the rigours of these early Daytona events, the 1940 race ended with only 15 of the original 77 starters still running!

In the last Daytona 200 before the USA's entry into the war, Canadian Billy Mathews created something of a sensation by winning the race on a British Norton at the record average speed of 78.08 mph – even though Mathews had 'decked' it, taking a mouthful of sand in the process. But he picked himself up and charged back through the field to victory.

The war brought an abrupt halt to professional motorcycle racing in the States and no Daytona races were run until 1947, when a record crowd of over 27,000 fans was on hand to see the 142 riders (also a record) do battle for the $1,000 first prize. After a battle royal, Johnny Sprieglhoff, an Indian rider from Milwaukee, Wisconsin (must have been a brave man to ride for the opposition when he hailed from the home town of Harley-Davidson!) won in 2

83
32
85

76

116
92

hours, 35 minutes and 33 seconds, an average speed of 77.14 mph. Tim Edwards (Indian) was second, with Harley-Davidson-mounted Alli Quattrocchi third.

Before the 1948 event was run, promoter Bill France (a former Daytona garage owner and stock car driver, and later owner of the Daytona International Speedway) moved the course down the beach a couple of miles – as part of the 'old' course was being affected by new housing development. The basic layout was the same but the length at 4.2 miles was longer with a clear, two mile run up to the two straightaways. A further point of interest is that the date of the Daytona Beach meeting varied year to year to coincide with the most favourable low tide times.

Floyd Emde (father of the 1972 winner Don) was the 1948 victor on an Indian, snatching the last success by this famous marque at Daytona. Emde Snr completed 49 laps (as did all of the first 20 finishers). His winning average speed of 84.01 mph was achieved in 2 hours, 22 minutes and 56 seconds.

Realising the potential of the American market and the selling power of Daytona successes, the British factories (notably Norton) began taking an interest in the Florida classic and top British tuners Steve Lancefield (1948) and Francis Beart (1949, '50 and '51) made the transatlantic journey to fettle the leading Norton machinery. Although a Manx Norton had finished second in both the 200 miler and the 100-mile amateur race in 1948, it was the following year which was to bring Daytona glory to the Birmingham, England marque.

On 13 March 1949 all records were smashed at Daytona. In the 200-mile National Championship Dick Klamfoth set a new race record of 86.42 mph when he took his Norton to victory in front of around 16,500 fans. Not only this but second and third placed men Billy Mathews and Tex Luse were also using Norton machinery. As if this wasn't

Left
Daytona 1952, Richard Brase (116) Triumph and Scott Rogers (92) Manx Norton, taking on fuel before the race; they were both early retirements

Below
View of pits area, 1953. The photograph captures the atmosphere of the period perfectly

Above

With the Norton threat ruled out by the AMA, the new Harley Davidson 750 KR side valve was victorious in the 1953 Daytona 200 miler. Paul Goldsmith won in 2 hours, 33 seconds, an average speed of 94.45 mph – a new record

Right

The first four men home in the 1958 200-miler were all on Harley-Davidsons. From left to right: winner Leonard, Mann (2nd), Morris (3rd), and Resweber (4th). Joe Leonard set a new record covering the distance in 1 hr 59 min 11 sec, at an average speed of 99.86 mph

enough Nortons also took first and second in the 100-mile Amateur event.

Norton then went on to scoop three more Daytona victories in successive years; Dick Klamfoth winning for them in 1951 and 1952 adding to his 1949 victory, whilst Canadian Billy Mathews won the 1950 200-miler – nine years after his first success. The final Norton victory was a truly disastrous one for the American made bikes, the first Harley-Davidson finishing way down in 15th place – their lowest ever position in the race, whilst the Indians were even farther off the pace.

All this was too much for American pride and the AMA authorities banned the over-the-counter Manx Norton racers, despite the fact that at 499 cc they were giving away half their capacity to the 750 cc Harley-Davidson and Indian racers. In fact a partial ban had been in force anyway with a compression ratio limit on all foreign-made bikes; whilst Norton were only allowed to use the old pre-1950 plunger frame and not the superior Featherbed chassis, even though the latter was fitted as standard equipment on Manx Nortons from 1951.

In the author's opinion the ban was a bit premature as Harley-Davidson were then in the process of developing their famous KR racer and a contest between the Manx Norton and the new Harleys would have been very close, the KR being vastly superior to the anachronistic WR model which it replaced. A witness to this theory is the fact that in 1953 Paul Goldsmith won on one of the new KR models and his average speed of 94.45 mph was considerably superior to Klamfoth's final Norton victory. Goldsmith also had the distinction of winning the last major car event on the beach course – the only man ever to win the main event on both two and four wheels.

Bobby Hill from Columbus, Ohio gained BSA their first Daytona 200 victory in 1954 when he headed a field of 107 riders to take the chequered flag in 2 hours, 7 minutes and 22.70 seconds – an average speed of 94.24 mph. The first five machines were all BSA, whilst the first American bike was Don Hutchinson's Harley back in 10th place.

But this was to be the last of the 'foreign' victories in the 200-miler, with Harley-Davidson taking over the proceedings to dominate the final six years of the

old beach circuit with Joe Leonard, later to become one of America's top stock car drivers, setting a record winnning average of 99.86 mph in 1958.

Half of these six victories went to Brad Andres of San Diego, California, who became 'King of the Beach' when he chalked up his third Daytona 200 win at an average speed of 98.06 mph on Sunday 13 March 1960 – the last in the series before the event was transferred to Bill France's new Daytona International Speedway.

In this final beach race the first fourteen home were all Harley mounted: Andres, Roeder, Leonard, Murquia, Ronald Emmick, Morris, Tibben, Buchannan, Schafer, Garry Emmick, O'Brien, Gholoson, White and Howell. The Harley-Davidson domination of the 200 mile beach race was complete, but one has to question how much of this was earned, rather than provided by the AMA rule book...

In a pattern which was to be transferred to the purpose-built International Daytona Speedway, supporting the main race on the traditional circuit were a number of motorcycling events over a full week. The standing start quarter mile sprint saw plenty of excitement in the big class. First a twin-

Left
Brad Andres winning the 1955 event; his race average speed was 94.57 mph

Bottom
Start of the 1958 200-miler

Below
Chuck Silverthorn (Harley-Davidson) leads Pat McHenry (Triumph) in the 1958 200-mile race. They finished 37th and 41st respectively

1

engined Triumph eliminated a 1,250 cc supercharged Harley. Then that particular Triumph was defeated by the eventual winner, another twin-engined Triumph which set a time of 10.81 seconds running on petrol.

A series of Lightweight races were run on a 1.7 mile airfield circuit and an interesting facet was that Italian ace, Francesco Villa, who had been 'imported' by the Ducati factory via their Stateside distributors, the Berliner Corporation, was not allowed to ride as he was deemed to be a professional racer and therefore did not qualify for the AMA 'Sportsman' class. However, in a special race Villa was beaten by Jim McLaughlin of Los Angeles riding a Parilla ... so much for the fear of works entries.

It is worth mentioning that the famous 200 mile beach/road circuit was getting near the end of its life – even if the new Daytona Speedway venue hadn't been available. Not only were there a number of substantial problems by 1960 ranging from local land use conflicts to the rapidly deteriorating condition of the road section, but the racing machinery was rapidly outgrowing the venue. As one era drew to a close, a new one was just about to begin...

Left
The winners enclosure after the 1958 Daytona 200 miler. Number 1 is the winning Harley-Davidson KR 750 ridden by Joe Leonard

Below
The top three finishers in the 1959 race. Left to right Tony Murguia (wearing HD jersey) 3rd, Brad Andres (with Trophy) 1st and Dick Mann (AMA jersey) 2nd. Time was fast running out for the 'Beach' venue

3
Catalina Island

The Island of Catalina lies some twenty-six miles west of Los Angeles and was the home of a very special form of motorcycle racing during much of the 1950s. The first 'Grand Prix' was staged there during a two-day meeting held over Saturday and Sunday 6/7 May 1951. The ten mile Catalina circuit was laid out by riders Aub Le Bard and Del Kuhn over a wide range of surfaces from street pavement to rock-strewn dirt track and everything in between – including part of the local golf course! The race meeting had as its base the picturesque small town of Avalon, itself immortalised in the music of the legendary band leader Benny Goodman.

An American journalist reporting the first Catalina races described Avalon and its surrounding area thus: 'Few human habitations on earth can boast of so great a charm. An assemblage of tidy white

Close racing as the Lightweight Class scream in for the finish in Avalon, only town on the island of Catalina. 1956 event shown, 66 is a 200 cc Triumph Cub, 50 a 175 cc MV Agusta

homes, gleaming in the midst of semi-tropical splendour, faced by the azure blue of the Pacific and sheltered by a cove recessed in the mountain range that rises precipitously from the ocean to comprise the island, it is one of the most pleasant spots on earth.' Catalina Island, situated as it was, bore some geographical comparison with the Isle of Man. While the Manx circuit could lay claim to be a race of a thousand gearchanges, Catalina's 100 mile 'Grand Prix' could counter as a race of a thousand turns.

The race itself was started on the main street of Avalon, fronting the ocean, and immediately after the drop of the flag the riders embarked on a 3½-mile 'grapevine' climb over crushed rock road topping the mountain ridge at an altitude of 1,900 ft. There followed an extremely narrow, serpentine, fire control road of rutted, rocky surface and maintained by the authorities only so far as to keep it passable. At points this section of the road clung precariously to the steep mountainside, with many hairpin turns on which to keep the nerve-ends at full stretch – a mistake could have truly frightening consequences.

The descent back to Avalon was over similar terrain, at points narrowing so that it was possible for only one motorcycle at a time. About a mile and a half of hard surface within the town limits completed the 10.3 mile course. A combination of road racing, scrambles (moto cross) and enduro riding skills were needed to be successful in this unique event.

At the first meeting British motorcylces predominated greatly, with an occasional native Harley or Indian v-twin, but in truth the much lighter European machinery held a distinct advantage as results would prove over the next few years.

The start procedure was that competitors would get underway in five-machine groups at half-minute intervals. Even so, their hurricane climb up through the narrow streets fairly rocked the houses to their foundations. Each succeeding wave added to the crescendo of excitement, so that spectators' breathing did not return to normal until the booming exhausts were reduced to a distant thunder in the mountains high above the town.

Early leader Nick Nicholson (BSA) eventually had to give way to the winner Walt Fulton (Triumph). The final result being Fulton, Chuck Minert (BSA), Del Kuhn (AJS), Nicholson, Wally Albright (AJS) and Ray Tanner (Harley-Davidson). The latter was the only runner in the first ten to be mounted on an American bike. The winner's time was 3 hrs, 30 mins, 16.91 secs.

The 100-mile race was, of course, the focal point of the meeting. However, earlier on Saturday 6 May, a 50-mile race for 125 and 250 cc machines was held over a shorter, less demanding 6-mile course (amounting to some 4 miles of pavement and 2 miles of dirt). The smaller class was won by Glen Clinton on an Austrian Puch split single two-stroke whilst Nicholson took the 250 cc event on an ohv BSA C11. The leading American bike in the 125 cc race was Tommy Bassari (Mustang) in 2nd, whilst Dick Hutchins took 4th (on a Harley) in the 250 cc category.

Tower Hill – three riders embark on the long downhill section. Note extremely loose surface; flint and granite stones abound. Leading machine is a BSA Gold Star

The 1952 meeting was dominated by BSA: Ray Weiman won the 50-mile 125 cc event on a Bantam; Nick Nicholson won the 50-mile 250 cc event; Aub le Bard won the 350 cc 50-miler; and Nicholson was the winner in the 100-mile open class on a 499 cc Gold

A disconsolate Indian rider, who has retired after he slid to earth, watches another competitor on a Harley-Davidson approach the summit of Tower Hill, circa 1956

Star. Nicholson's victory came from a total of 204 riders in the main event which was open to all engines up to 1300 cc. The only race not won by BSA was the 200 cc class, in which not a single Beeza was entered.

On to 1953, and the open class 100-miler was won by John McLaughlin riding a 350 pushrod Velocette entered by dealer Lou Branch. The same rider also took the 250 cc event, riding another Branch tuned Velo. In the latter event an Italian Moto Guzzi finished second. The 200 cc went to Ray Adams (Francis Barnett) whilst the 125 cc race was won by Dave Ekins riding an NSU Fox.

The year 1954 saw the AMA (American Motorcycle Association) refuse to allow the meeting to carry a national title as the bikes did not adhere to the organisation's Class C specifications. At Catalina, any machine was allowed to compete regardless of make, model, compression ratio or any home-brewed modification, as long as it was judged to be safe. A Velocette machine again won the open class event, this time Jimmy Johnson on a 499 cc single. But Harley-Davidson had their best year yet with the big Milwaukee v-twins taking 2nd, 6th, 7th and 10th places.

There were now five lightweight classes: 125 cc two-stroke was won by NSU; 165 cc two-stroke by Harley-Davidson; 150 cc ohv & 200 cc two-stroke by Zündapp; 250 cc sv & two-stroke, Puch; 269 cc sv & 255 cc ohv, BSA. Finally, in the 21 cu in (350 cc) class, Dave Ekins took an ohc NSU to victory.

The growing importance with which the Catalina races were now being seen is confirmed by the presence of the engineer Fritz Kocheise, who came over for the races from the NSU factory in Germany to look after the company's products, including the specially prepared 250 Max ridden by Ekins.

In 1955 it was the turn of Dave Ekins' elder brother Bud to taste a Catalina victory. This time however it was the big one, Bud completed the 100-miler in 3 hrs, 8 mins, 49.17 secs, breaking the record set by Johnson the previous year by over 10 minutes. Ekins was riding a 649 cc Triumph Trophy. Interestingly the third-placed machine was a Harley v-twin ridden by Long Beach motorcycle policeman, Russ Good, but this was after several of the most fancied runners had been either forced out through mechanical trouble or crashes.

If 1955 had been the year of Bud Ekins and Triumph, 1956 was very much the year of the BSA Gold Star, with examples ridden by Chuck Minert, Walt Axtelm and Charlie Wheat grabbing the top three placings in the big race. The main lightweight race was won by Ed Kretz Jnr. on a 199 cc Triumph Cub, who saw off a huge variety of machinery from the likes of Harley-Davidson, Maico and even MV Agusta.

On the 4th and 5th of May 1957 the seventh two-day Catalina Grand Prix meeting took place. British machines filled the first twelve places in the open class in which there were 199 starters and 100 finishers. In the opening stages Bud Ekins and Bob Sandgren, both on Triumph Trophys, headed the field, riding within a minute of each other. But rear wheel trouble dropped Ekins from the lead to eighth at the finish, leaving victory to Sandgren.

The same man and machine won in 1958 – Sandgren becoming the first rider to score two open class Catalina victories. Chief opposition again came from Bud Ekins, who, for the first few laps, equalled Sandgren's lap times. Ekins' effort was soon eliminated by a split oil tank on his 500 Triumph.

The 1958 lightweight events provided almost as much excitement as the big race and were made all the more interesting by the apperance of five 250 cc Yamahas, one ridden by the Japanese star Fumio Ito, who eventually finished sixth. The race was won by a Puch, whilst the 200 cc class went to a Triumph, 175 cc to MV and 125 cc to NSU, the lightweights providing a truly international selection.

Thereafter the Catalina event went downhill rapidly and didn't survive into the 1960s. But in the period covered here it was always in the top handful of 'race' meetings staged in the USA, thanks to its location and unique format.

As a footnote, the combination of Fumio Ito and Yamaha were the first all-Japanese team to compete in the States; but not the Americas as a whole, this honour being reserved for a works prepared 125 cc Honda, ridden by Mikio Omura, at Sáo Paulo, Brazil in February 1954 (see *Classic Japanese Racing Motorcycles* Osprey Publishing).

Below
Catalina GP 1958. Open class winner Bob Sandgren (10) Triumph TR6 passes Jack Baldwin (21) BSA, Don Thompson (175) Triumph and Jim Hood (103) Triumph. By winning this event Sandgren became the only man to score two open class Catalina victories

Overleaf
Catalina June 1958. Open class gets under way with hot pre-race favourite Bud Ekins (22) well to the fore. But rear wheel trouble dropped Ekins from an early lead to eighth at the finish

AMBULANCE
24
22

33
27
26
25
28
20

4

The Harley Saga

Harley-Davidson's early racing history is charted in Chapter 1, and I have chosen the year 1952 as my starting point for the Milwaukee factory's post Second World War story. The reason for this is the famous Model K which was debuted that year, and represented the most extensive redesign ever carried out by the house of Harley-Davidson on their venerable v-twin concept. Although it retained the side valve 750 cc configuration of the earlier W series, much else was totally new; including unit construction of the engine, gearbox and clutch assemblies, foot gearshift, a double loop cradle frame, swinging arm rear suspension and, last but not least, telescopic front forks.

In addition to the basic roadster line, the new K generation was also offered as the KRTT road racer/TT model and the KR rigid-framed flat tracker. However, the competition models were not available until August 1952, the result being that the K-series didn't really get started in serious competition until the following year.

Technically the racing KRTT/KR engines differed from their roadster brothers in detail rather than basics. For example whereas they employed the same bore and stroke, same crankcase and cylinder barrels, the racer had ball bearings instead of a mixture of roller bearings and bushes. It also featured lumpier cam profiles, larger valves, a competition magneto and a special exhaust. As for power output the standard roadster produced 30 bhp, the racer between 40–42 bhp (later this was to be upped to well over 60 bhp!).

The high point of the 1953 Harley-Davidson racing effort was without doubt Paul Goldsmith's victory in the prestigious Daytona 200 on his KR, at a

Five-man works Harley-Davidson team before the start of the 1953 Daytona 200-mile race

new record average speed of 94.45 mph, which came after several years of British victories (bikes, not riders) in the legendary event.

A special off-road competition model intended for scrambling and desert racing, the KRM, was built. But this proved uncompetitive, being too heavy to succeed against the more nimble British 500 cc singles and 650 cc vertical twins.

The 1954 Daytona 200-miler saw a reverse of the American v-twins fortunes, with BSA taking the first five places at Daytona, a feat not repeated until the rise of Yamaha some two decades later. However, British bike fans were to be disappointed as the rest of the AMA's racing season was dominated by Joe Leonard, riding a Harley KR. Leonard won eight out of a total of 18 events in the 1954 championship season, including the Laconia 100. Joe Leonard was also the first man to become AMA National Champion on his cumulative season record, rather than a single race as had been the practice in previous years.

An important factor in Leonard's success was the tuning ability of Tom Sifton. Formerly a San José motorcycle dealer Sifton had sold out in August 1953 so as to be able to concentrate on his real love, that of

Paul Goldsmith winner of the 1953 Daytona 200 miler and top man that year in the Harley team

tuning engines. Sifton's tuning expertise gave Leonard an engine which produced around 50 bhp at the rear wheel – outstanding for a 750 side valver in the early 1950s. His main efforts to boost power went into porting the cylinders, improving cam profiles and fitting dual coil valve springs, the latter from the noted Triumph expert, Tom Witham. Other improvements concerned sodium filled valves, chrome-plated stainless piston rings and the use of 5/16 inch big-end rollers in place of the original smaller diameter 3/16 inch components. The latter modification was later adopted by Harley-Davidson themselves.

At the end of the 1954 season, Tom Sifton was persuaded to part with his super special KR Leonard motor, in fact he sold the complete machine to his friend and Harley-Davidson dealer, Leonard Andres. Andres' son Brad was then about to start his first season in the AMA expert ratings. The Sifton-tuned ex-Leonard bike proved its worth by assisting the 19-year-old Andres junior to win the 1955 Daytona 200-miler at a record average speed of

Left
John Gibson Harley-Davidson winner of the 1956 Daytona 200 mile race, his only National victory that year

Right
Joe Leonard (seated) and Everett Brasher; two members of the 1957 Harley-Davidson factory team

94.57 mph. Brad Andres went on to win several other events on the AMA championship trail, including the Laconia '100', Dodge City '75' and the legendary Langhorne '100'; emerging at the season's end as the AMA No 1 plate holder – the only 'rookie' ever to have done so. Everett Brasher was second, with Joe Leonard third. All three were Harley-Davidson mounted, in fact only two events in the 17 round series went to non-Harley-Davidson riders that year.

This level of success brought about a change in the rule book in November 1955; at their annual conference AMA officials voted to allow the maximum allowable compression ratio for the following season to be raised from 8:1 to 9:1, a decision which only helped Harley's main British rivals. It should be noted that the KRs were then running a compression ratio in the region of 6.5:1.

The compression ratio allowance proved of little help to the opposition as the 1956 season was to reveal – Harley-Davidson machinery taking all seven title rounds. Although Joe Leonard won only two, the Mile at San Mateo, California and the TT at Peoria, Illinois, he still amassed enough points to reclaim the AMA No 1 from Brad Andres who finished second in the championship race.

It was that man Leonard again in 1957, winning not only the championship but half of the eight races, including his first Daytona 200 victory. For a change his nearest challenger was not another Harley man, but Al Gunter (later to win fame on four wheels in Indianapolis-style racing). Gunter rode a 499 cc ohv BSA Gold Star; another Beeza rider, Dick Klamfoth was third. Most noteworthy to our story was the emergence of Carroll Resweber who finished fourth; his points tally including two National victories: the half-miles at Columbus, Ohio and St Paul, Minnesota. The year 1957 also saw veteran Harley-Davidson race chief Hank Syvertson retire, to be replaced by Dick (OB) O'Brien.

The following year, 1958, Carroll Resweber was champion, a position he was to hold for a record breaking four seasons in a row, all on Harley-Davidson machinery. However, that first year's title was anything but easy, Resweber scoring 36 points to Joe Leonard's 35 . . . and the former champion was sidelined for half the season through injury. This was to be a familiar pattern over the next few years, Resweber taking the championship, Leonard running him close.

As for the foreign invaders, BSA was the main challenger to Harley-Davidson supremacy, with its Gold Star singles and 650 twins scoring several individual National victories.

During Resweber's reign (1958–1961) Harley's other leading riders (besides Joe Leonard) were Brad Andres, Everett Brasher, Duane Buchanan, Troy Lee, Bart Markel and Roger Reiman. The last two individuals were both destined to become future AMA champions.

April 1960 brought news of a merger between the Italian Aermacchi company and the Milwaukee factory. This gave Harley-Davidson the chance to market (and race) Aermacchi bikes in the USA.

The 1962 season got underway with Don Burnett winning the coveted Daytona 200-miler on a 500 Triumph twin; ending a string of seven consecutive Harley-Davidson victories in this famous event. The year's AMA champion was 27-year-old Bart Markel from Flint, Michigan. Bart took over from Carroll Resweber when the four time champ was involved in an horrific accident at the Lincoln, Illinois 5-mile championship race in September. At that time Resweber led Markel 44 points to 40 and it had appeared that Resweber was heading for his fifth consecutive No 1 plate. But this was not to be. Jack Goulsen, Dick Klamfoth and Resweber all went down heavily during a practice lap. Goulsen was killed instantly, Resweber injured a leg so severely that he was destined never to race again and Klamfoth was so sickened after the experience that he hung up his leathers there and then. Markel went on to take the title with 58 points, Resweber's tally staying on 44; then came Dick Mann riding a combination of BSA (Gold Star) and Matchless (G50) machinery.

Dick Mann was champion in 1963 – but only after a lot of bitter controversy (covered in Chapter 9) concerning his Matchless G50. Mann took the title by a single point from Harley-Davidson teamsters George Roeder and Ralph White.

The rising popularity of small capacity bikes led to a 250 cc AMA National Championship. The 1963 event was staged at the Peoria, Illinois TT circuit. Bart Markel won, riding a Harley (read Aermacchi) ohv Sprint. *Cycle World* tested both the Sprint and the latest KR (actually the Jerry Branch tuned machines raced by Dick Hammer). Both sported dolphin fairings, which AMA had allowed from the beginning of that year in road racing events. The Sprint achieved 116 mph, the KR 142 mph. Prices for the 'standard' over-the-counter racers were $900 and $1,295 respectively, and power output figures were quoted as: Sprint, 28.5 bhp @ 9,500 rpm; KR, 48 bhp @ 6,800 rpm.

The Sprint, later to be raced in the States in 350 cc as well as 250 cc form, kept Aermacchi's lightweight chances alive for some years, most notably in the AMA Expert Class short track ($\frac{1}{4}$-mile) racing. But once the Japanese Yamaha twins became reliable as

Harley rider Tony Murguia changing gear by hand during the 1960 Daytona 200 – he still managed to finish 4th. His machine is the latest version of the KR750 side valve model

well as quick (from the mid 1960s onwards) the Sprint's fortunes waned in road racing events. The full development history of the Sprint is charted in the Aermacchi section of *Classic Italian Racing Motorcycles* (Osprey Publishing).

1964 again saw Harley-Davidson back on top of the AMA's championship pile, this time the rider was Roger Reiman; his two victories in the seventeen round series came at Daytona and the Short Track meeting at Hinsdale, Illinois. Reiman gained his title, as Mann had done the previous year, on consistency, rather than outright race wins.

Roger Reiman scored his second consecutive Daytona 200 victory in March 1965, but in the season long AMA championship series it was Bart Markel who upheld Harley's honour against a flood of British bikes from BSA, Triumph and Matchless; whilst Dick Mann became the first rider of a Japanese machine to win an AMA National, when he took his Yamaha TD1B twin to victory in the 250 cc race at Nelson Ledges, Ohio. It was also the first time a two-stroke had won an AMA National.

Markel was again No 1 in 1966, carried to success aboard the latest version of the long-running KR side-valver. But generally the American marque had a tough year with Triumph machinery taking many of the honours, including victory at Daytona. One

Dick Hammer from Lakewood, California rode for Harley-Davidson during most of the 1960s; his best year was 1963 when he finished 5th in the AMA National Championship

A KR750 side valve racer at Daytona in 1967

Above
Cal Rayborn (25) Harley-Davidson KR750 during the 1967 Daytona 200 miler, he finished 5th

Below
Engine details of 1967 KR750 racer. Rear cylinder, head, piston and gudgeon pin ...

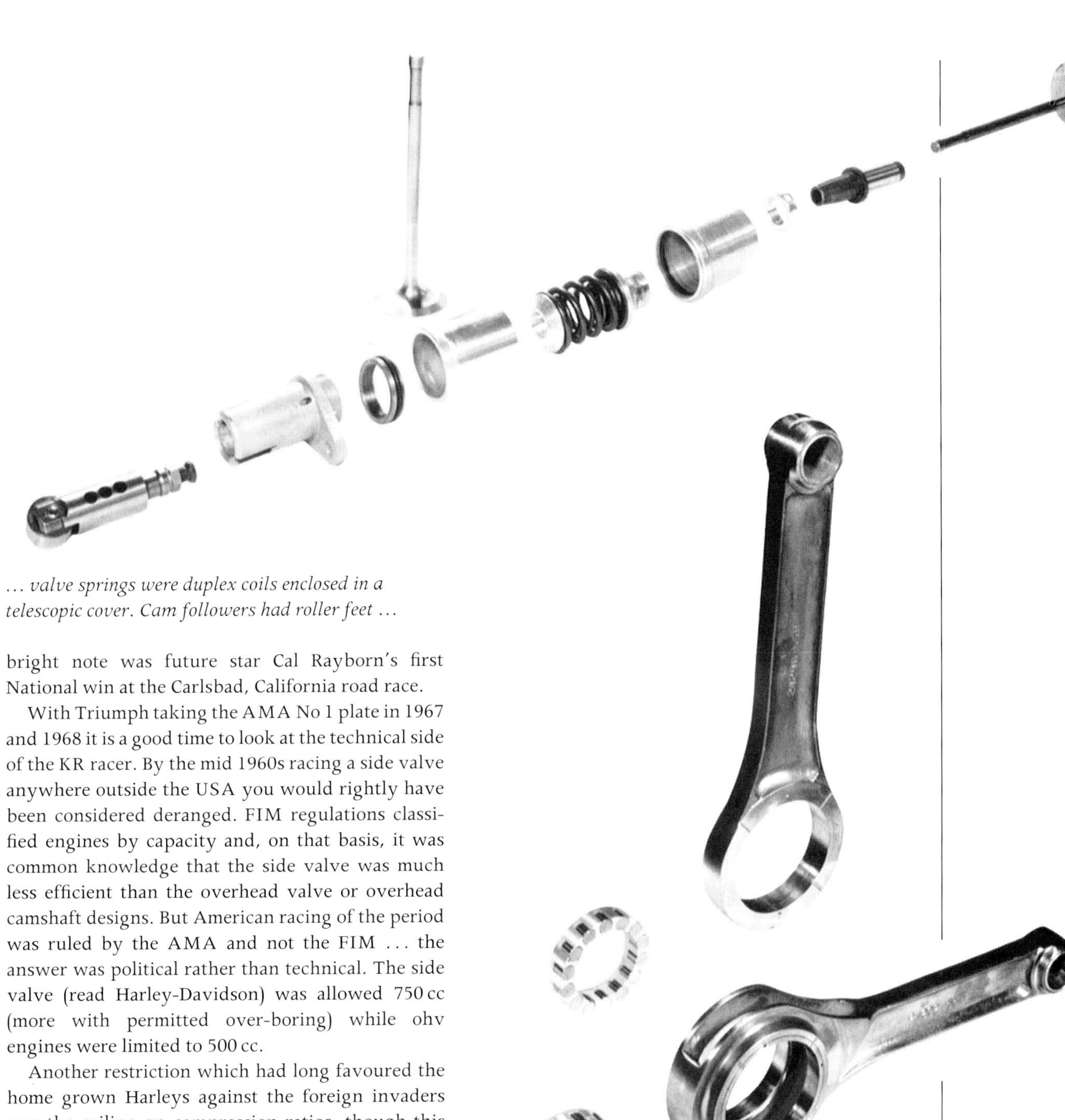

... valve springs were duplex coils enclosed in a telescopic cover. Cam followers had roller feet ...

bright note was future star Cal Rayborn's first National win at the Carlsbad, California road race.

With Triumph taking the AMA No 1 plate in 1967 and 1968 it is a good time to look at the technical side of the KR racer. By the mid 1960s racing a side valve anywhere outside the USA you would rightly have been considered deranged. FIM regulations classified engines by capacity and, on that basis, it was common knowledge that the side valve was much less efficient than the overhead valve or overhead camshaft designs. But American racing of the period was ruled by the AMA and not the FIM ... the answer was political rather than technical. The side valve (read Harley-Davidson) was allowed 750 cc (more with permitted over-boring) while ohv engines were limited to 500 cc.

Another restriction which had long favoured the home grown Harleys against the foreign invaders was the ceiling on compression ratios, though this had been allowed to slowly climb from 7.5:1 to 9:1 over the previous two decades. The lower figure was just about as high a ratio as could be squeezed from a tuned side valve, with its large, sprawling valve pocket at the side of the cylinder head; but it blunted the edge of a British production racer just enough to help Harley's cause.

Even so getting a side valve 750 through the speed traps at around 145 mph was still a marvellous achievement, especially when one considers the technical problems in tuning a side valve for speed work. For starters there is the tortuous layout of the induction tract and the masking of the valve head,

... con-rods, caged big-end rollers and single crankpin ...

both of which seriously impair cylinder filling. The high ratio of surface area to volume in the combustion space means that a good deal of heat is dissipated instead of being put to work. Finally the casting of the (cold) inlet and (hot) exhaust ports alongside and integral with the cylinder bore brings severe distortion problems.

The 45-degree v-twin had a capacity of 741 cc (69.77 × 96.84 mm) and after the first 150 miles the cylinders were rebored (not honed) to the first oversize to combat the effects of distortion; otherwise oil consumption was alarmingly high and power reduced between 4 and 8 bhp! Maximum oversize permitted by AMA regulations was 0.045 in. giving a capacity of 767 cc.

Four separate camshafts were employed and each was carried in two ball race bearings, one at each end. Valve timing figures (with standard factory over-the-counter cams) were as follows: inlet opens 66 deg before tdc, closes 66 deg after bdc; exhaust opens 58 deg before bdc, closes 42 deg after tdc.

... contour of the inlet port (larger of the two) was critical; it was hand finished. No gasket was used at the cylinder head joint. Sealing was effected by a thin coat of metallic aluminium paint ...

The contour of the inlet port was critical to the KR's performance, and was always hand finished, even on the 'production' examples. No gasket was used at the cylinder head joint. Sealing was effected by a thin coat of metallic aluminium paint.

Except that the discs were steel forgings, the design of the crankshaft flywheels and connecting rod assembly was reminiscent of vintage bikes of the 1920s. The $1\frac{1}{2}$-inch (38 mm) diameter crankpin and both mainshafts were clamped against steep tapers and keyed. The assembly was carried in a ball bearing in each half of the crankcase. The big-end eye of the rear cylinder connecting rod was forked to accommodate the front conrod, the bearing comprising three rows of $\frac{5}{16}$ inch (8 mm) diameter caged rollers. Valve springs were duplex coils enclosed in telescopic covers. Cam followers had roller feet. Valve head diameters were: inlet $1\frac{7}{8}$ inch (48 mm); exhaust $1\frac{5}{8}$ inch (42 mm).

In road guise the KR sported swinging arm rear suspension with damper units of the gas cell type to prevent aeration of the hydraulic fluid. Both drum brakes were $8 \times 1\frac{1}{2}$ inch (205 × 38 mm) of the single leading shoe variety. Ignition was taken care of by a Fairbanks Morse rotating-magnet magneto. Breathing through a large air filter, the standard carbur-

... four separate camshafts were used and each was carried in two ball bearings, one at each end ...

ation set up was a single $1\frac{15}{16}$ inch (33 mm) Linkert, later replaced by a $1\frac{1}{2}$ inch (38 mm) floatless Tillotson diaphragm instrument.

To cater for the various forms of racing, there were wide choices of tanks, tyres, wheel rims, hubs, seats, handlebars and rear suspension (some events such as flat track even employed a different frame with a rigid rear end). A wide range of sprockets provided for a variation in top gear from 2.95 all the way through to 10.03:1 and there were a total of ten different four-speed gear clusters, depending upon the circuit.

As for performance, in the trim sold by Harley-Davidson to its customers the 1966 KR750 road racer produced 48 bhp (at the rear wheel) with the engine spinning at 6,600 rpm. Crankshaft rating was around 53 bhp, the works models turning out another 10 bhp.

A one-off 883 cc ohv XLR Sportster engine was

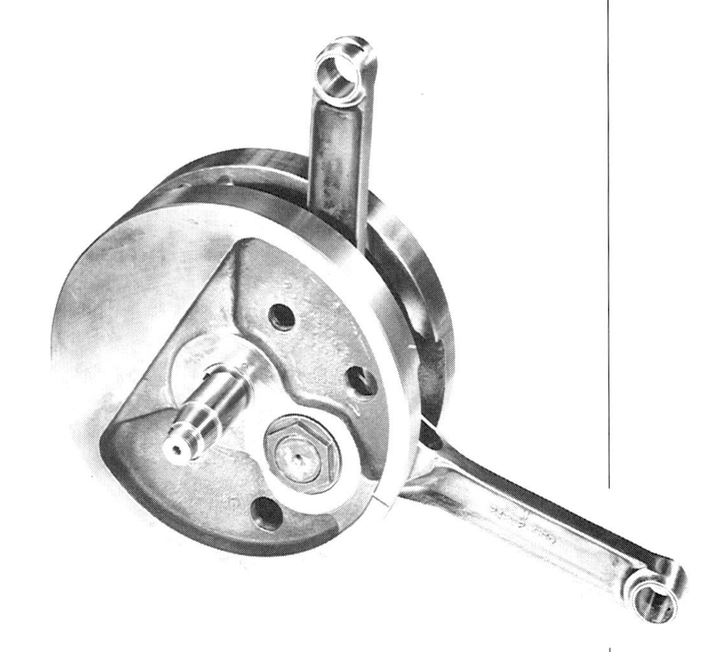

... massive crankshaft assembly from 45 degree v-twin engine

Engine from Weil's machine: 883 cc (75.8 x 98mm) ohv, with cast iron cylinder barrels and heads. Maximum power 70 bhp @ 7,000 rpm

fitted into a special 'Low-boy' frame and raced by the Californian Lance Weil on British short circuits during 1967. It won 1,000 cc races at Lydden Hill, Brands Hatch, Oulton Park and Mallory Park, and in the process created a considerable amount of publicity on both sides of the Atlantic.

After its defeats by Triumph during 1967 Harley-Davidson made an amazing come back to the AMA racing scene with a revitalised KR model for 1968/9. This was due to the whole of 1967 being spent by Dick O'Brien and his team of engineers in gleaning yet more from the venerable side valve design. For a start there was now a 'Low-boy' frame of the type used on Weil's machine and special accessories such as tank, seat and most important of all a wind tunnel-tested fairing; these latter components being the work of the Wixom Bros of Long Beach, California. Although Dick O'Brien never revealed the exact power output figures for the revised 1968 works KR, they were considerably improved . . . probably well over 60 bhp at the rear wheel with the rpm now up to over 7,000.

Known improvements include *twin* Tillotson diaphragm carburettors, revised exhaust valve timing and new cam profiles. Also because of the new twin carb arrangement the combustion chambers and compression ratio were both altered. Proof of how effective this work had been is to realise that Harley gained some 8 mph on lap speeds at Daytona, with Roger Reiman setting the fastest qualifying speed for the 1968 200 miler at 149.080 mph. In the race Cal Rayborn went on to lap all but second and third by the end of forty laps, furthermore he also became the first rider to win the event at an average speed of over 100 mph.

Only eight KR750s were built for 1969 – all team bikes. They all employed Italian Ceriani front forks and massive Fontana four leading shoe front drum brakes, with an American-made single hydraulically operated disc at the rear.

Cal Rayborn again dominated the proceedings at Daytona and the majority of the other road races that year, but it was fellow Harley-Davidson rider Mert Lawwill who took the championship with 672 points, thanks to his flat track skills. Rayborn finished third in the title rankings with 517 points.

But 1969 was also to see both the end of the KR era (the AMA were introducing a new more open 750 category for 1970) *and* the company taken over by the giant AMF corporation (American Machine and Foundry Group). As the new decade dawned the Harley-Davidson race shop headed by Dick O'Brien was faced with some real headaches, brought about by the new set of AMA rules and the fact that AMF although interested in raising the production of the standard roadster line didn't see racing as a priority. Even so O'Brien tried. The result was first shown to the public at the Houston Show, Texas in February 1970 . . . it was the XR750, designed by Dutchman Pieter Zylstra.

The prototype was built within a four month period. This short time and the fact that although supposedly a new design it owed much to the old KR side valve (cycle parts) and the standard production XL Sportster (engine assembly). Lined up against machines such as the BSA/Triumph triples, the Honda CB750 four and the Ducati v-twin, the 'new' Harley was obviously going to find life difficult.

A major problem with the original XR750 was that the racer retained the roadster XL's cast iron barrels and heads (obviously modified and tuned). Why? One can only assume economy and the need to get the bike out on the track as soon as possible. Even the forged piston blanks came from a known source, this time the Offenhauser 1500 cc four cylinder midget racing car engine, which by chance (or was it design?) shared the same 76 mm bore and 82 mm stroke, which gave the XR750 a capacity of 748 cc.

Initially, the compression ratio was 9.5:1, but this was subsequently lowered, first to 9:1, and then to

Above
Single Tillotson carburettor with diaphragm fuel-flow regulator

Below
Nearside view of the Weil 883 cc XLR-TT racer, showing oil tank, chrome plated primary chain case, full duplex frame and Fairbanks Morse magneto

Above
Front end of the Cycle World *sponsored 883 cc Harley-Davidson as raced by Lance Weil was all-Italian with Aermacchi handlebars, Ceriani forks and a 240 mm ($9\frac{1}{2}$-inch) 2LS double sided front brake from the same source. But stopping the heavyweight Harley proved too much for the Italian brake and it was later replaced by a Lyster double-disc assembly*

8.4:1 in an attempt to combat overheating problems. The engine had a wider spread of power than the old KR side valver, whilst team manager O'Brien stated the power output to be '62 bhp at 6,200 rpm' – but failed to say whether this was at the crankshaft or rear wheel. And anyway anything less than 70 bhp in 1970 and you might just as well have walked.

Overheating was to prove a truly massive problem and as many as four separate oil coolers were fitted to the works bikes at Daytona in 1970 – but to no avail as all the XRs retired! The highest placed Harley was a faithful KR side valver down in sixth place.

The Daytona race exemplified the 1970 season; that is, total disaster. Officially Harley-Davidson blamed piston failures. But the troubles were not that simple and far more widespread. And most of these centred around too much heat. The 'iron' XR750 motor soon gained a none too happy nickname, the 'Waffle Iron'. And this was to be the prime cause of team bike breakdowns during the championship season with god-awful regularity. Of the 25 races counting towards the AMA title Harley-Davidson only won seven – defending champion

Below
Harley-Davidson race chief Dick O'Brien – the man responsible for much of the factory's success during the 'classic' era

Right
Cal Rayborn seated on the new XR750 ohv racers at the start of the 1970 Daytona 200. Unfortunately for Rayborn and the rest of his teammates the new design (soon nicknamed 'Waffle Iron') suffered serious overheating problems causing his retirement on the 40th lap of the race

CAL
25

Above
The 1971 version of the XR750 had twin Japanese Mikuni carburettors in a specially fabricated heat shield; this was an attempt to isolate the instruments from the excessive heat generated by the engine. Note also one of the giant oil coolers

Left
Harley camp, Daytona March 1971. The only Milwaukee finisher in the top twenty that year was Roger Reiman who brought his XR750 home in 4th spot, a lap behind the winner

Mert Lawwill eventually finished sixth, the best of the Milwaukee teamsters. This was also the company's lowest ever finish in the National championship.

During the closed season break O'Brien and his men carried out a mini-redesign, with reworked cylinder heads, new crank flywheels (forged steel and with the mainshaft also forged as an integral part of the flywheel); the heads were now held in place with long through studs into the crankcases, instead of separate bolts from case to barrel and from barrel to head. But any gain made to the engine was offset by a spate of gearbox breakages, certainly for the first half of the 1971 season.

In road racing events Cal Rayborn showed himself to be a true master of the craft, at least whilst his bike kept going. Even though he was down on speed he rode like no one else in Stateside road racing during 1970 and 1971. How sick he must have been with his machinery, which in those two years broke down nine times out of ten. But the old 'Waffle Iron' did have one weekend of glory, when Rayborn amazed the British by winning three of the six Anglo-American Match Races during Easter 1972 on an iron XR750 prepared by Walt Faulk (see Chapter 10).

Something had to be done, and that something was the new alloy engined XR750; which appeared in time for the 1972 season. Unfortunately for Cal Rayborn and Harley-Davidson the large capacity Japanese two-strokes, not to mention the new wave European 750 four-strokes were by this time also on the American scene in great numbers. There were now Yamaha, Kawasaki and Suzuki strokers, in addition to the four-strokes such as the BSA/Triumph triples.

The first the world saw (and it was only a glimpse) of the prototype alloy engined XR was at the Ontario circuit in October 1971. Then it was tucked away inside the big Harley-Davidson race transporter. Before Ontario, this engine had been tested on a one-mile dirt track, but never on any sort of road course. However, Harley's Dick O'Brien told members of the press that the team intended to stay on at Ontario after the meeting so that Rayborn and Brelsford could make tests.

The alloy engined XR750 had new short-stroke bore and stroke dimensions of 79.5 × 75.5 mm giving

BELL
7
CHAMPION
7

a capacity of 749.5 cc. Compared with the iron engine the alloy job had a much more robust bottom end. The $1\frac{1}{2}$-inch (38 mm) diameter crankpin was now integral with the driveside flywheel, and the connecting rods were an inch shorter. An immediate advantage of the new alloy top end was its much improved cooling, this also allowed the compression ratio to be boosted from 8.4 to 10.4:1. The alloy engine was also 17 lb (8 kg) lighter, which not only gave a better power-to-weight ratio, but, as the decrease in weight was at the top end, the centre of gravity was also lowered.

Finally with some 80 bhp at 8,000 rpm available, the 1972 XR750 was considerably more powerful, giving a maximum speed approaching 165 mph on optimum gearing; not quite in the 100 bhp two-stroke league but a vast improvement over the 1970/71 iron engine. Reliability was also much improved, but there was still the odd glitch or two.

Left
The only AMA National road race to be won by Harley-Davidson during 1971 was Mark Brelsford's victory at Loudon, New Hampshire; for once the Waffle Iron kept its 'cool' long enough to win

Below
A new much modified alloy-engined XR750 appeared in time for the 1972 season. It not only ran cooler, but was also much more robust and more powerful

One centred around the valve gear. This had been 'borrowed' from the Aermacchi ohv flat single. When employed on the Italian bike it was used with the camshaft linked directly between crankshaft and rockers; but with the Harley v-twin, the four one lobe camshafts were splayed and the pushrods were not parallel to the bores. Nor were they parallel to each other, while the inlet rockers had the valves inboard of their shafts and the exhausts were outboard. This meant there were different angles between the valve stems and the cam lobes . . . putting the system which worked well on the Aermacchi single simply didn't work on the v-twin.

None of this was realised when the initial design was carried out. Soon however the exhaust cams were having to be modified and a spate of broken rocker arms began to occur. This was eventually cured through a redesign of certain components, the rocker arms included.

There were also more minor problems concerning

oil and ignition systems and pistons; but these were all solved relatively quickly. Not so the intended five-speed transmission. Several gear clusters were built and tested, but in the end Harley-Davidson gave up. The reason? Well, when you try and put five pairs of gears in a compartment that used to have four, you have reduced their width (and strength!) by some 20 per cent. That is also the reason why it hasn't been done since and probably never will be on an XR engine.

Besides riders such as Rayborn and Brelsford, Harley were also able to call on the services of the Italian star Renzo Pasolini, thanks to the Aermacchi connection. Pasolini proved himself a quick learner and although Kawasaki won the important Ontario F750 event (run in two heats, due to concerns over tyre wear) Pasolini was Harley's best result with third overall.

After Rayborn's superb showing in the 1972 Easter Match Races he returned to England that September for the Race of the Year at Mallory Park. This time he had one of the latest model alloy engined XR750s and full factory support (something he didn't have for his original visit). In the race he duelled with Yamaha works GP star Jarno Saarinen until the Harley's magneto expired.

After the lean years of 1970 and 1971 when Harley-Davidson failed miserably, 1972 was generally a good year, with Mark Brelsford becoming the new AMA National Champion. The Harley rider scored a total of 1483 points; nearest challenger was Triumph-mounted Gary Scott on 1105. Other leading contenders that year included Gene Romero (Triumph), Kenny Roberts (Yamaha), Chuck Palmgren (Yamaha), Dick Mann (BSA), Jim Rice (BSA) plus the Harley trio of Mert Lawwill, Cal Rayborn and Dave Sehl.

The following year was to prove a poor season for the American factory. Out on the road, its thundering ohv v-twins were totally outclassed by the latest crop of Japanese machinery, whilst even on the dirt

Right

The Italian star Renzo Pasolini was drafted into the squad for the 1972 Ontario F750 races – he proved his worth by gaining Harley's best result at the meeting with third overall

Below

The alloy engined XR750 had new short-stroke dimensions of 79.5 x 75.5 mm, giving a capacity of 749.5 cc. Machine shown is Mert Lawwill's, Ontario, 1 October 1972

the combination of Kenny Roberts and the Yamaha XS650 vertical twin proved a serious threat to the Harley's former invincibility in this branch of the sport. Proof of Roberts' influence is to recall that in winning the AMA title he scored a total of 2014 points compared to his nearest rival Gary Scott's 1241, with the third place going to Gary Nixon with 887.

Typical of the 1973 season for Harley was the Daytona 200. Brelsford who had qualified at 97.954 mph (Rayborn's qualifying speed was 98.503 mph) suffered a truly awful accident on lap 11 of the race in which he sustained two broken legs, a broken hand and badly damaged kneecap, which sidelined the AMA 1972 Grand Champion for the rest of the year.

Below
'Paso' cranking his XR750 near the limit at Ontario. Sadly he was to be killed the following year in a horrific crash during the 250 cc Italian GP at Monza

Overleaf
Mark Brelsford of Woodside, California took the 1972 AMA Grand National title with a total of 1483 points. Although shown here on an XR750 road racer, he was best on the dirt in Half-mile and TT events

Harley-Davids

Mert Lawwill
GOODYEAR
LAWWILL
7

Left
Harley teamster Mert Lawwill signals a 'blown engine' in the first race of the F750 class at Ontario, October 1973

Above
Brelsford (right) with HD race chief Dick O'Brien at Daytona in March 1973

Later in the race Rayborn's engine seized, throwing him off the bike. In the incident he landed heavily, breaking his collarbone and suffering damaged ribs. Cal came back too soon – his collarbone not fully mended, and another incident where he got into a 'tank slapper' only aggravated things. History records that he went to England as captain of the USA team against the Brits; what most people don't know is that he rode with the still broken collarbone and was in considerable pain.

1973 was a terrible year for Harley-Davidson, particularly in road racing where the faster and much lighter two-strokes were so much more competitive. Even Rayborn's undoubted skill couldn't make the difference. Rayborn was so frustrated by this state of affairs that he quit Harley-Davidson at the end of that year. Tragically the 33-year-old Californian was to be killed whilst having his first outing on an 500 cc Suzuki twin when he crashed at the Auckland, New Zealand circuit on 1 January 1974. The Suzuki had been loaned to Rayborn so that he could compete in an international series being sponsored in New Zealand by the Marlboro tobacco company. He was also due to have driven a Lola in racing car events during his stay in the country.

Many informed observers consider Cal Rayborn to have been America's finest road racer of the pre-Grand Prix era and the precursor of riders such as Roberts, Spencer, Lawson, Rainey and Schwanz. Probably his most courageous ride of all was when he established a new world motorcycle speed record at the Bonneville Salt Flats (see Chapter 8) in the autumn of 1970. With virtually no forward vision in the cramped cockpit into which he was fitted flat on his back, he still clocked a world beating average speed of 265.492 mph. Certainly Calvin Rayborn was Harley-Davidson's finest road racer of all time, and a great sportsman to boot.

Following Rayborn's departure and subsequent fatal accident the Milwaukee factory never again repeated its former road racing successes, and except for Battle of the Twins racing in the 1980s never gained another Daytona victory. (This statement is made taking into account that the four world titles in the mid 1970s were gained not by the American Harley-Davidson effort, but by the Italian Aermacchi

Right
Streamlining used on the 1972/73 XR750. Note also Ceriani forks and Japanese brake calipers

Below
An XR750 on show in Britain during the late 1970s. It's the actual bike raced to 3rd spot by Renzo Pasolini at Ontario in October 1972

John A Davidson, President of Harley-Davidson, opening 'On Track' show at Daytona Hilton Hotel, 9 March 1977. Left to right Kim Roussea, Walter Villa, John Davidson, Jay Springsteen and Mary Park

branch, with an Italian rider, so falling outside the scope of this particular book).

Harley-Davidson still produced its share of AMA champions once Kenny Roberts had departed to Europe. These were: 1975 Gary Scott; 1976, 77, 78 Jay Springsteen; 1979 Steve Eklund; 1980 Randy Goss. But all these victories were performances in flat track and TT type events, not in road racing.

Even so credit must be given to the supreme ability in these branches of American racing by that legend of the late 1970s, Jay Springsteen. 'Springer' as he was popularly known, had that rare talent as displayed by the likes of Leonard, Resweber and Markel in earlier days, of a fearless ability to put his Harley v-twin in front of the pack and stay there until the chequered flag.

No other manufacturer comes anywhere near Harley-Davidson's record in AMA racing; they were to America what MV Agusta were to Europe in the classic period from 1945 until the end of the 1970s. That famous No 1 emblem really was carved with sweat, blood and tears in true American fashion.

5
Desert Racing

During the late 1950s, throughout the 1960s and into the early 1970s desert racing (akin to an enduro event but over vast distances) flourished in the Western United States and Mexico, where there are huge areas of desolate cowboy-style wastelands. However the sport disappeared as rapidly as it had started in the late 1970s as government bodies began to take heed of the environmental lobby.

Competitors taking part in the 1958 Big Bear Run. The course embraced 150 miles of scrub and sand in the vast Mojave Desert, California

Two of the most famous desert races were the Big Bear Run and the Baja. The first took place in the Mojave Desert – only an hour's drive from the urban sprawl of Los Angeles. The Mojave is 400 square miles of uninterrupted nothingness, in places unbelievably rough, but in other parts pretty smooth, with a sort of 'washboard' effect on the surface and with small scrub bushes, some two feet high, growing in it. However there are also areas which are positively crawling with hazards for the speeding motorcyclist – yucca trees three feet in diameter anchored to the desert floor as if set in concrete,

masses of cactus and deep ravines. On top of these dangers, there is the temperature to consider – around 110 degrees farenheit in the shade during the summer months – except that 'shade' doesn't exist out in the desert!

But the Big Bear Run – probably America's most famous cross country race – could be even more hazardous. Usually held at the beginning of the year, in January, it could trace its history right back to the vintage and veteran days of motorcycling. A description of the 1956 event, the 35th 'Big Bear', provides an insight into the event.

Staged by the Orange County Club on California's Pacific seaboard, the Run took competitors through a 151-mile course over snow, mud, extensive stretches of sand in the Mojave Desert and many miles of narrow, dusty fire roads. The fire roads were emergency tracks in the hills to provide access to forest fires. Riding conditions favoured British rather than American machines, the lighter weight and easier handling of the former making them less tiring to ride.

The tremendous toll of men and machines can be imagined when one realises that of the original 626 starters only 92 riders completed the course within the prescribed time limit. With such a vast entry, the organisers expected no challenge to their claim that

Start of an American desert race; hundreds of bikes often took part

the Big Bear Run was 'the world's largest motorised race'.

The 1956 event was won by Bill Postal riding one of the then new 649 cc Triumph TR6 Trophy's, as did the second and third finishers Bud Ekins and Arvin Cox. Class winners were: 250 cc Glen Clinton (Zündapp), 200 cc Gene Mondrick (Dot), 165 cc Bob Skipsead (Triumph), 125 cc Bud Watkins (Ducati). Postal's winning time for the race was 4 hours 7 mins.

The other truly great desert race was the Baja (pronounced Bah-Ha) 1000. Run in Mexico the first event took place in 1966. Organised entirely by, and primarily for, the Americans, it traversed the narrow peninsula of desolate land comprising mountain, scrub, desert, pine forest and jungle that points due south from the border into the Pacific. When it was first run there was little but dirt tracks between the shabby shanty border crossing at Tijuana and the southern city of La Paz. Then it was a true 1000-mile blind race from one to the other, with competitors using what passed as highway and any other land, dodging other traffic and local populace alike, for 20 hours.

Later in the 1970s a proper tarmac highway was

Above
A Triumph rider wading a river during the 1962 Jack Pine Enduro

Right
Harley-Davidson advertisement proclaiming the success gained by its Italian built SR100 two-stroke in the Baja desert race, circa early 1970s

constructed, and the organisers of the Baja were forced to revise their course to cover more barren ground. This led to a shorter, 1000 kilometre (around 600 miles) circuit taking a giant oval loop starting from Ensenada, just south of Tijuana and returning there. Although shorter, this new course was much, much tougher than the original. (It still survives to this day, but the vast majority of competitors now use four-wheel drive cars and trucks). Riders of special note included Malcolm Smith (who did much of the riding in the 1971 film *On any Sunday*), Mitch Mayes and Larry Roeseler.

As for the machinery used, several specially prepared Swedish Husqvarnas of either 360 or 450 cc won, together with a series of Harley-Davidson two-strokes built at the Italian Aermacchi factory. But the great mass of Baja bikes were of Japanese manufacture, with the odd British bike thrown in for good measure.

Another famous American enduro type race was the spectacular annual Barstow to Las Vegas Run which entailed several hundred riders starting in a single line and racing across 500 miles of open desert from California to the Nevada border. However, strong environmental pressure led the Californian State Government to ban the event following a study into the damage done to this section of the desert floor by such a large number of machines. The result was that this particular wasteland is now preserved as a national heritage park and the AMA and other organising bodies were forced to adopt a staggered start system to minimise the wheel-track decimation.

The ecologists did have a point, of course, and it is important to realise that American deserts are not a 'sea of sand' like the North African type. Instead they generally comprise a covering of coarse, tough vegetation. By the late 1970s the environmental

The Yank that took on Mexico and won.
The Harley-Davidson SR-100.
Our trail-bustin' 2-stroke single with a 9.5:1 ratio, five-speed box, Ceriani forks and shocks. The SR beat most of the best at the worst.
With a string of wins that's outta sight: Mexican 1000. Baja 500. California desert races. Motocross. Scrambles. Hare 'n hounds.
Put on your riding gear, then grab yourself some freedom on a Harley-Davidson SR-100.
We'll be content to rest on your laurels.
Harley-Davidson,
Milwaukee, Wisconsin 53201
Member Motorcycle Industry Council
AMF
Harley-Davidson
Harley-Davidson SR-100.
The Great American Freedom Machine.

lobby had grown in strength to the point where even the Mexican government had begun to make influential noises on their behalf. This was to sound the death knell for the long distance desert endurance scene, which today is all but gone. Now only memories remain of the time when motorcyclists could roam the vast expanses of the American wastelands, as the cowboys did in days gone by.

During the mid 1970s Harley campaigned specially prepared versions of the SX250 trail bike with considerable success in the Baja event; motocross version shown.

6
Dirt Track

One form of motorcycle sport is more 'American' than any other – dirt track racing (or flat track as it is often called). At first glance, Stateside dirt track competition and speedway racing might appear to follow similar patterns but the only real parallel between the two is that in each case the action takes place on dirt ovals. But otherwise the racing programme and riding styles are so dramatically opposed that the only similarities between a dirt tracker and a speedway iron are the use of two wheels and the handlebar bend.

Early this century when powered two wheelers became sophisticated enough for use in competiton events, board track racing became popular in North America; tracks being specially constructed for racing with both four and two wheels and spectators flocked to see this form of sport in their droves. Yet the actual racing remained somewhat impractical to say the least. The tracks were not only expensive to erect and maintain, but also difficult to relocate. The fledgling racers began to cast a covetous eye towards the myriad mile and half mile dirt tracks then used

Ever since the pioneer days of American motorcycle racing, dirt track events have been an integral part of the scene. Here a group of riders dual for the lead on one of 1-mile ovals in the late 1950s; a Harley-Davidson KR750 is leading the pack

24
24

Above
Sacramento, California Mile Track. Gary Nixon (9) Triumph, Dick Mann (2) BSA and Dick Hammer (16) Harley-Davidson dispute the lead during a 1967 event

Left
The side-valve KR750 Harley-Davidson of National Number 24 Jack O'Brien of Los Angeles, California in 1960. (His tarmac racer is shown)

exclusively for horse racing across the length and breadth of the USA.

And so as the 1920s passed, board racing disappeared from the scene to be replaced by competition on the oval horse race tracks, which were soon reverberating to the echoes of thundering Indian and Harley-Davidson v-twins. Virtually every local horse track was soon playing host to the motorcycle racing fraternity. At this stage the sport was still primitive and it was a common sight to see competitors riding their bike to the course, racing it, and, if everything was still in one piece (including the rider), riding it home after the racing programme had been concluded.

In these early days there was little or no prize money available and the would-be 'stars' did it for the love of the sport and precious little else. There was also a very special camaraderie between the competitors. If one struck trouble there was always someone only too ready to provide help.

The rise of dirt track racing continued into the 1930s, although the Great Depression acted as a brake at the beginning of the new decade. This was mirrored by the sport of speedway racing in the USA during the same period. With a large band of loyal and fanatical fans, speedway enjoyed something of a boom. American riders were often as good as anyone: the Californian star Jack Milne became World Speedway Champion in 1937.

Both dirt track and speedway suffered greatly from the cessation of activities during the Second World War. When the conflict finally came to an end, dirt track racing made a successful recovery, but not so speedway which in America languished as a sport until the 1970s when riders such as Bruce Penhall, Scott Autrey and the Moran brothers re-established Americans as world class competitors.

When dirt track racing resumed in 1946, it did so with many young riders unheard of by the fans. A few pre-war stars remained, notably Chet Dykgraff, but it took several years for a new band of riders to become household names.

One major change from the pre-war to post-war period was a stricter set of rules and regulations.

XR
HARLEY-DAVIDSON 750

XR
750 AMF HARLEY-DAVIDSON

Left
One of the greatest dirt racers of all time the 1972 XR750 Harley-Davidson ...

Below left
... looking purposeful in every line ...

Right
... alloy cylinder barrels and heads, twin spark magneto, dual high level pipes ...

... Ceriani forks, pull-back 'bars, massive air filters and 45 degree v-twin engine, it could only be an XR750 flat-tracker

Brelsford and Harley-Davidson – a formidable combination of skill and power respectively

'Bouncing Bob' the legendary Ascot Park flagman, September 1972

Before the war, each dirt track had its own set of rules, and some didn't have any at all! This was because the meetings were mainly organised by the local Indian and Harley-Davidson dealers. These men usually organised things to suit their own riders. Tales of races continuing for just as long as it took for the local favourite to emerge as the front runner and victory were commonplace ... The tracks were also almost always either 'Indian' or 'Harley' and if one of the rival marque's won, things could get out of hand, with open warfare amongst the spectators.

Establishment of the AMA (American Motorcycle Association) in 1923 began a trend towards standardised rules, but it was not until the end of the Second World War that the regulations were enforced on a truly national basis.

Along with the resumption of racing in 1946 came the idea of a national champion. From 1946 until the 1953 season, this champion was determined by a single race, the prestigious 25 laps of the 1 mile Springfield, Illinois dirt oval. It was the veteran Chet Dykgraff who took the very first official American title by scoring a superb victory on his

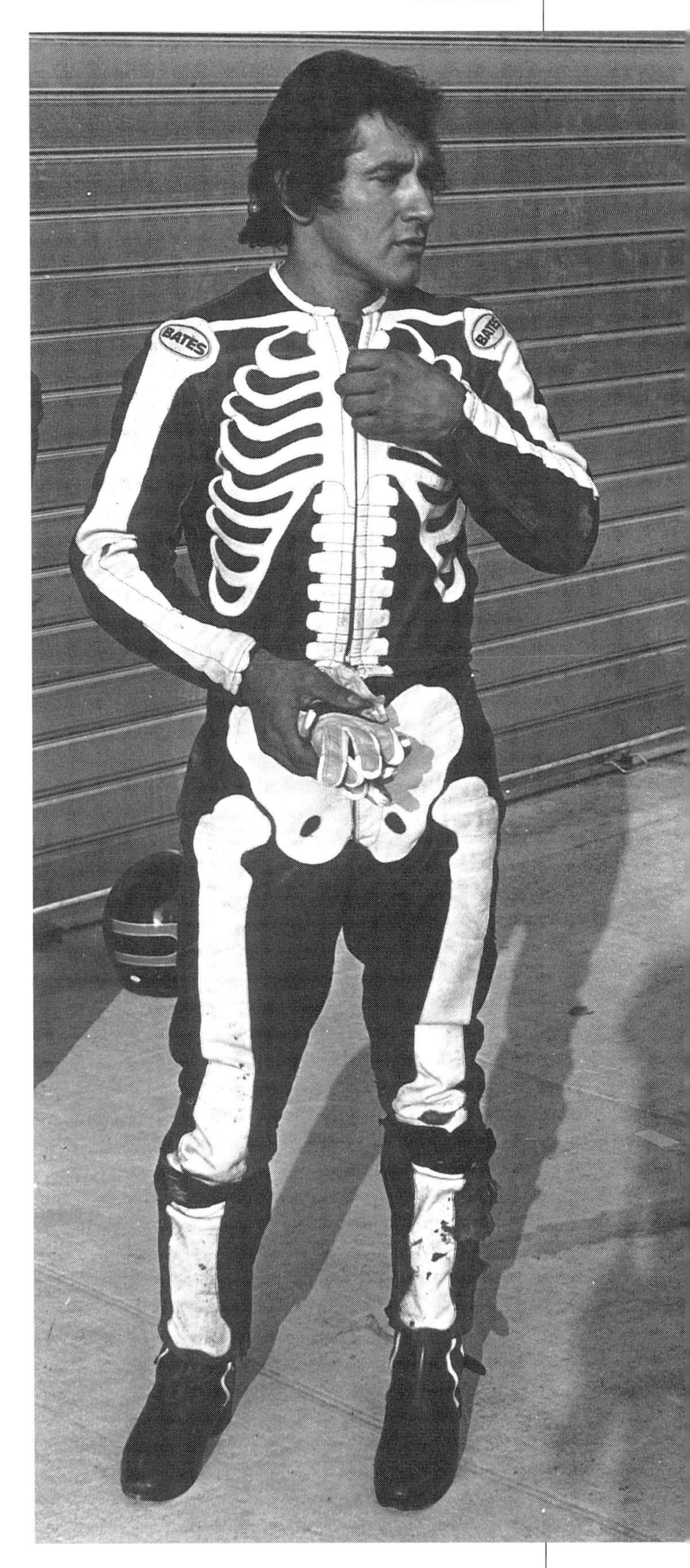

Right
Dave Aldana created a massive stir when he appeared in these skeleton leathers during the 1970s

British Norton overhead cam single at Springfield in 1946.

This victory really annoyed the two remaining American big-time manufacturers, Harley-Davidson and Indian. The former responded by providing the winning machinery for the next three seasons in the very capable hands of Jimmy Chann. In 1950, Larry Headrick on yet another Harley took victory at Springfield and with it the coveted No 1 plate for the following twelve months.

Next it was the turn of the super-smooth rider Bobby Hill, who scored back-to-back championships in 1951 and 1952. Finally came a win by the experienced Bill Tuman, who took his thundering Indian v-twin to victory in the last single race ever to decide the American national title at the Springfield oval in 1953. For 1954 the AMA introduced a new championship format whereby the result was decided over a series of races throughout the season.

The first AMA Grand National title chase was destined to be one of the most closely fought in the history of the sport, with 'Smokey Joe' Leonard eventually emerging as the highest points scorer. Leonard, who was to find fame on both two and four wheels, also went on to capture the championship again in 1954, 1956 and 1957. In a long, distinguished career, Smokey Joe stacked up a grand total of 27 national victories, a number unsurpassed until the advent of the legendary Bart Markel many years later. In addition to his ability to ride fast, Leonard also displayed a versatility which was to prove absolutely essential in AMA racing, because, as recounted in greater detail in Chapter 7, the Grand National Series was beyond doubt the greatest test of versatility in the whole of motor sport.

Originally five types of racing made up the series. One was America's own stone-age version of road racing – in which the combatants campaigned standard issue dirt track irons and even dragged their feet through the turns! The other four types of racing were half-mile, mile, short track and, most exciting of all, the TT Steeplechase. The latter (no relation to the Isle of Man TT) comprised both right and left turns, plus a mighty jump which saw the riders shoot 30 or 40 feet at speeds often well in excess of the magic ton.

For short track events, engine sizes varied through the years before finally settling at a standard 250 cc maximum. Other types of dirt track racing were open to two classes originally 45 and 80 cubic inch. But before long, rules for the national series were standardised and the maximum engine capacity was set at 750 cc. As with speedway, the machines had *no* brakes (rear brakes were allowed from 1970). As a result, the racing was quite unique, and with speeds of over 120 mph on the longer tracks, exciting in the extreme . . . imagine a massive Harley v-twin drifting sideways and broadside at three figure speeds. Full lock broadsides were needed to scrub off speed in lieu of braking equipment.

Up to the end of 1960s Harley-Davidson, with their side valve 750 cc v-twins and the Italian built 250 cc ohv Sprints were usually the front runners, with British bikes led by Triumph never far behind. The full story of the Harley involvement is catalogued in Chapter 4.

With the advent of the 1970s the new ohv XR750 Harley appeared, together with a fresh set of challengers from Japan and Europe. In the big class, the Harley-Davidsons and Triumphs were joined by the first of the serious Japanese dirt track irons, the Yamaha XS650 dohc twin. And in the lightweight

Below
Yamaha XS650 dohc twin as campaigned by Roberts; this is the final version

category the top bikes were all two strokes; Champion KTM, Champion Can Am, Ossa ST-1 and Bultaco Astro.

As for the riders themselves Leonard was succeeded by Carroll Resweber as top dirt dog during the late 1950s. But it is still worth recalling that Leonard moved on to twice win the National United States Auto Club title for Indianapolis type cars, making him one of only a handful of men around the world who have successfully switched from bikes to cars including John Surtees, Mike Hailwood and more recently Johnny Cecotto.

Harley teamster Resweber won four consecutive titles in 1958, '59, '60 and '61. He might have won more had not a serious accident in 1962 forced his early retirement from the sport. 'Bad Bart' Markel was the next dirt track ace, not only winning the 1962 AMA title, but also taking the championship in 1965 and 1966.

Dick 'Budsy' Mann was very much an all-around specialist proving equally good at other branches of the sport which went to make up the championship trail, including road racing. Mann was champion in 1963 and then again in 1971.

Above
Yamaha mounted Kenny Roberts (1) hounds Harley rider Mert Lawwill at an American dirt track oval in 1974, Roberts was equally good on dirt or tarmac

Overleaf
Squad of Harley-Davidson XR750s dispute the lead during the late 1970s; Number 1 is the legendary Jay Springsteen

Roger Reiman only scored a single title, in 1964. Gary Nixon should have won more than his back-to-back titles in 1967 and 1968, but serious injuries were to plague his career.

Mert Lawwill and Gene Romero were both single holders of the AMA crown – in 1969 and 1970 respectively – as was Mark Brelsford in 1972. The latter could more than likely have repeated his success had not a crash at the following year's Daytona road race and a leg fracture with near fatal complications ended another outstanding career prematurely. The young Kenny Roberts was the undoubted star of the 1973 and 1974 seasons (see Chapter 11), with triple runner up Garry Scott taking the title in 1975.

1
12
TED
62

72
42

The year 1975 proved to be one of the closest fought with Scott scoring 1358 points, against Roberts' 1260 and newcomer Jay Springsteen's 1027. The following year saw Springsteen, then still only 19 years old, become one of the youngest champions ever in the AMA title chase. He achieved his success by winning seven National events on the dirt in only his second season on the National circuit. Springsteen went on to take the title many times thereafter including 1977 and 1978. Others who became champions during the period covered by this book are Steve Eklund (1979) and Randy Goss (1980).

Those who never became title holders, but never-

Left

During the late 1970s and early 1980s Jay Springsteen was the undisputed master of the American flat track ovals and TT events on his works XR750 HD ...

Above

... these three views give some idea of the style ...

Right

... and the technique which made 'Springer' such a great champion.

theless deserve a mention include Cal Rayborn, Sammy Tanner and Eddie Mulder. Although Rayborn was mainly a pavement artist, the other two were leading contenders on the dirt track scene. As for venues, there were scores. But the pick of the bunch included: Ascot Park, Gardenia, Los Angeles; Castle Rock, Washington; Peoria, Illinois; Lincoln, Illinois; Columbus, Ohio; Elkhorn, Wisconsin; Phoenix, Arizona; and Sacramento, California.

Finally there is no doubt that without dirt track racing expertise it was *impossible* to become the AMA champion from the end of the Second World War until the end of the 1970s . . . in other words the 'Classic' era. Dirt track racing was that important to the American racing scene.

7
AMA

The AMA (American Motorcycle Association) is the most powerful organising body in motorcycle sport outside the FIM (Federation Internationale Motorcycliste); and certainly the biggest and busiest national federation in the two wheel world with its activities spanning a wide spectrum from Youth Division off-road riding to professional road racing.

The AMA was formed in 1923 to take over responsibility for promoting and organising the sport in the USA in place of the virtually extinct Federation of American Motorcyclists (FAM). The FAM had been torn asunder by internal disagreement over a debate concerning professional versus amateur status, with no-one able to make a firm decision.

Enter the AMA. One of its first moves was to phase out the use of exotic works machines in favour of the 'Class C' professional racing. Class C was intended to produce closer racing with its production-based formula. Not only did AMA officials see this as a way of keeping down rider's costs, but also of

An AMA accredited pressman questions Dan Richards after the Harley-Davidson rider had won the 1955 Daytona 100-mile Amateur Race

Roger Reiman (third from left) after winning the very first AMA sanctioned race – the 1961 Daytona 200 – to be held at the new International Speedway venue

encouraging brand loyalty – the spectator being able to associate the machine he rode on the street with the bikes being campaigned on the race track.

The basic AMA C Class ruling was that one started with a standard bike and modified it for racing purposes. A minimum of 100 machines of a particular type must have been made, it couldn't have more than two cylinders, and a 750 cc side valve was regarded as the equivalent of a 500 cc ohv model. The weakness, as manufacturers such as Harley-Davidson (and to a lesser degree Triumph) were to prove, was that the rider with the money and the determination to win will always find his way around whatever basic rules you care to make.

Class C was also intended to create the AMA racer as an extremely competent all round motorcyclist. He had to be, riding virtually everything from road racing to enduros. This system's weakness was that no one rider was allowed to develop to the ultimate in a single field. And, in the writer's opinion, this held back American riders until the AMA finally teamed up with the FIM in the 1970s.

Take the typical Harley-Davidson works team of the 1950s and 1960s. To beat the AMA system they usually ran a six or seven man team which had to include specialists in each field, but in practice each rider wanted to do well in all the competition events in the championship calendar, so it resulted in a watering down of excellence.

The basic venue for American motorcycle competition was the $\frac{1}{2}$-mile or 1-mile oval, with the wealth of fairground horse tracks encouraging the development of flat-tracking as the major Stateside motorcycle sport. The venues spread across the whole of the USA and produced close and fiercely contested racing. In addition, TT Steeplechasing added another dimension to the flat-track theme by introducing at least one major jump as well as left and right hand corners into the course layout.

The competition had a uniquely American flavour, and was quite unlike anything seen in Europe where road racing was considered the premier two-wheel sport. The nearest thing to European style racing was the annual Laconia, New Hampshire meeting which was staged over closed public roads. But long before Laconia's 1938 inception (see Chapter 1) and many years after the event's demise the AMA hierarchy displayed a marked reluctance to join with other countries competing under the umbrella of the FIM. In fact it was not until the early 1970s that the AMA became affiliated to the international body, and then only after much political intrigue and

infighting amongst the various AMA senior officials who were either for or against the idea. For the period covered by this book the AMA headquarters were based in Westerville, Ohio.

Immediately before and after the Second World War the Harley-Davidson concern was almost alone in supporting the AMA – without its support the organisation could well have floundered and gone to the wall. This explains in part the set of rules which were seen by many as very much favouring America's most important two wheel manufacturer from 1945 until the end of the 1960s.

In fact, Harley-Davidson nominated, and thereby

Left
However, the first motorcycle race meeting to be staged at Daytona International Speedway was an FIM affair; Englishman Tony Godfrey is seen here after winning the 500 cc race on a Manx Norton, a machine which had been banned by the AMA in the early 1950s

Below
For many years the Lightweight class at AMA meetings was dominated by the humble pushrod 200 cc Triumph Cub; here a competitor is shown at Laconia in June 1961

Dick Mann piloting the Matchless G50 dirt tracker which helped him win the 1963 AMA National Championship title. However, as they had done before the AMA reacted by banning the British ohc single from future events

effectively controlled, the full-time AMA official for much of this period, so it is little wonder that it followed the Harley line of restricting the sport to a very narrow band of rules. Also to be expected was that this often caused friction. There are several examples such as banning the dohc Manx Nortons in the early 1950s, the Californian importers of Triumph machines attempting to take that state out of the AMA and into the FIM in 1955, and finally the banning of the Matchless G50 in the early 1960s.

Throughout the 1950s and for much of the 1960s the AMA seemed more interested in maintaining the status quo and keeping foreign influence at bay, rather than promoting the sport and broadening its interest. Faced with this, splinter groups began to emerge, intent on promoting European style racing. Two of these organisations were the AFM (American Federation of Motorcyclists) and the AAMRR (American Amateur Motorcycle Road Racing).

But the 'real' conflict of interests was between the Swiss based FIM and the AMA. The FIM first gained a foothold albeit extremely small, through the USMC (United States Motorcycling Club). Formed by Tom Galen and Bill Tuthill this organisation had no full time staff and no facilities, but its creators were still able to convince the mandarins of the FIM that a working arrangement was in the interests of both parties. Given the green light to organise international meetings, the USMC discovered that they shared common goals with the Daytona International Speedway authorities who wished to move the AMA sanctioned Daytona 200 from the beach circuit to their new purpose-built track facilities and transform it into a real road race. The Daytona Speedway authorities realised that a USMC/FIM event could be just the spur to creating pukka European style racing in the States.

The inaugural FIM-approved road race in the USA took place on Sunday 12 February 1961. Stars of this Daytona event were Mike Hailwood, Tony Godfrey and the Japanese rider Moto Kitano. In shirt sleeve weather, a 12,000 crowd lined the new Daytona International Speedway for their first glimpse of European-style racing. And it was style which proved the decisive factor. For though European machines were in the majority, the bulk of the home riders employed the 'hot-shoe' technique of trailing the inside foot on corners – and so couldn't match the classic style of the British riders or Kitano (fifth in the 1960 Isle of Man Lightweight TT).

During practice Godfrey (on a G50 Matchless) had turned in the fastest 500 cc lap at 92.9 mph and at the fall of the flag on race day he left the field trailing – except for Hailwood (Manx Norton). In close company they circled the 3.1 mile lap; then, after three laps, Hailwood edged to the front. Godfrey came again and so it went on with the pair giving almost an exhibition way ahead of the rest. On the 12th lap Hailwood's ignition cut dead and for the remainder of the 40 laps Godfrey was unchallenged. The Englishman's winning average was 90.62 mph. Second was Buddy Parriott on a Norton and third Don Burnett on another G50 Matchless.

Measuring 1.66 miles to the lap and excluding the banked turn, a short circuit was laid out for the 38 lap 250 cc race. Informed onlookers hardly expected the works Honda four of Kitano to be seriously challenged but Hailwood riding a single cylinder dohc Mondial never eased the pressure. He stayed with the Japanese star from start to finish, whilst third finisher Luis Garon of Guatemala (NSU) was well out of the hunt.

Ironically, by the time the USMC-inspired FIM-sanctioned 'Grand Prix' took place the AMA had

Typical AMA approved 'racing' bike of the mid 1960s, the BSA A50 twin of 1963. Unlike the earlier Gold Star single, it wasn't really a threat to the domestic Harleys. In fact it could be classed 'AMA friendly'

also decided to stage its own events at the new Daytona circuit. The first such AMA race at the venue was contested by a band of 54 competitors; Harley-Davidson teamster Roger Reiman contested the lead with Carroll Resweber for the first 50 laps until Resweber was forced out with gearbox problems. Dick Mann was the only other rider in contention but a burnt out clutch sidelined him. Twenty-seven riders were still running when the final lap began and Reiman took the flag finishing 43 seconds ahead of Burnett (Triumph). George Roeder was third.

Mike Hailwood and Tony Godfrey returned to compete in the second United States Grand Prix in February 1962. Both riders were on Manx Nortons but neither finished. Fellow Englishman Ron Grant (later to settle in the USA) then moved ahead, but was also to strike mechanical problems. Honda factory rider Kunimitsu Takahashi then took over the leading position which he held to the flag. Jim Hayes and Dave Hetzler (both riding Nortons) were second and third respectively. This was Takahashi's third victory; he had also won the 50 cc and 250 cc races on works Hondas.

Japanese bikes also dominated the 1963 USGP; the Yamaha RD56 making an impressive debut, where, ridden by Fumio Ito, it won the 250 cc class, breaking the 1962 250 cc race record by one minute 29 seconds. Fellow Yamaha teamster Don Vesco rode an RD56 in the 500 cc event, winning by a full lap. The Nortons of Lance Weil and Roger Beaumont came home second and third respectively.

AMA Grand National Champion in 1967 and 1968, Gary Nixon

Following on from this in 1964 and 1965 there were two USGPs counting towards the FIM Championship series. However both suffered from a lack of spectators and produced a series of rows between the top riders and the organisers. This resulted in the USMC eventually going broke and a new body called the International Motorcycling Board of the USA carrying the FIM banner in the States. Subsequently the new organisation's title was changed to the Motorcycling International Committee of the United States (MICUS) with its headquarters at the Daytona Speedway and with active support from the AFM, AAMRR and others.

MICUS was to prove very slow to get off the ground and made very little real impression on the

Mert Lawwill broke Nixon's winning sequence by taking the title in 1969

MARK
CHAMPION
W-1
ARLEY-DAVIDS
BRELSFORD
Harley-Davidson
CHAMPION
1
1
Number six.
Nearly every cycle buff knows that Mark Brelsford won the AMA Grand National Championship in 1972. And the right to carry AMA's number one plate for 1973.
But did you know that this is the sixth straight year that the Grand National Champion has been fired to victory by Champion spark plugs? Mark's Champion-sparked predecessors include Gary Nixon, who took the title in '67 and '68, Mert Lawwill, the '69 winner, Gene Romero in '70, and Dick Mann in '71.
Harley-Davidson-riding Mark neatly wrapped up his championship with two more Nationals still to be run. He scored firsts at the 25-lap TT National at Ascot, the Louisville half-mile National and the half-mile National at Salem, Oregon.
Mark's brother, Scott, made 1972 the year of the Brelsfords. Scott rode his H-D to victory in six Junior Nationals, and earned the unofficial title: Top AMA Junior.
One thing both winning Brelsfords do is see that their Harley-Davidsons are fitted with Champion spark plugs. The brand that's right for every bike.
Better plugs for everyone
DEPENDABLE
CHAMPION
SPARK PLUGS
Toledo, Ohio 43601

Above
With its left and right turns and high flying jumps AMA TT dirt track racing was perhaps the most spectacular of all American motorcycle sports

Left
The Number 1 plate awarded to the AMA National Champion was worth a pot of gold to the advertising men, witnessed by this 1973 Champion Spark Plugs advertisement proclaiming six long years of Champion success

American motorcycling scene although it did manage to upset many AMA officials. Much of this centred around the fact that the AMA had been making overtures to the FIM, only to be told that since only one affiliation per country could claim FIM membership, the AMA would have to wait in line behind MICUS.

Nevertheless this situation led to a bizarre compromise, hammered out at the 1969 FIM Congress in Yugoslavia, whereby the AMA and MICUS would share FIM affiliation and responsibility for staging international events. Amongst other things the AMA and MICUS agreed to a 50–50 split in FIM events scheduled for the USA. Neither organisation would issue national or international licences to the other party's professional riders. Some saw this as an ideal compromise. However in practice the pact was to prove far from ideal . . .

In fact by the beginning of 1971 it had become clear that the AMA had abrogated the 'treaty' – if indeed one had ever existed to be ratified. One event, the Daytona 200, was back as a national status event after being international for 1970. Conversely things were not quite as clear cut as it might have appeared; the AMA deciding to throw in its lot with the FIM, providing a face-saving formula could be found.

And it was duly forthcoming: the AMA would trade unequivocal acceptance of FIM authority for international recognition of its linch pin, the Class C racing formula.

During the negotiation process Britain's ACU (Auto Cycle Union) played a vital part – it proposed changing Class C into 'Formula 750'. This idea proved acceptable to both the AMA and the FIM; the result being that the AMA became an important segment in the ranks of the FIM. The broadening of the AMA's international horizon coincided with a tremendous upswing in its fortunes at home. Membership shooting up by almost double – from 108,000 at the end of 1970 to over 200,000 by mid 1972.

The following year the AMA successfully staged the world famous ISDT (International Six Days Trial) in the Berkshire Hills around Dalton, Massachusetts. Originally the plan was to hold the event in the state of Texas, but officials considered that conditions would be too dry and dusty. By 1977, the AMA produced its first World Champion; appropriately this was in the Formula 750 road racing category, the rider being Steve Baker.

Since that time the AMA has licensed riders such as Kenny Roberts, Freddie Spencer, Eddie Lawson

Right
Arena racing action – fast and furious

Below
Arena racing (short rack) was usually contested with machines with a maximum capacity of 250cc. Popular engines in the 1970s included Bultaco, Can-Am and Harley-Davidson

Postwar AMA national champions

1946	Chet Dykgraff
1947	Jimmy Chann
1948	Jimmy Chann
1949	Jimmy Chann
1950	Larry Headrick
1951	Bobby Hill
1952	Bobby Hill
1953	Bill Tuman
1954	Joe Leonard
1955	Brad Andres
1956	Joe Leonard
1957	Joe Leonard
1958	Carroll Resweber
1959	Carroll Resweber
1960	Carroll Resweber
1961	Carroll Resweber
1962	Bart Markel
1963	Dick Mann
1964	Roger Reiman
1965	Bart Markel

Overleaf
Randy Goss the 1980 AMA champion; like Springsteen he rode Harley-Davidsons and most of his success came on the dirt, not the tarmac

and Wayne Rainey all of whom have won the blue riband of motorcycle sport, the 500 cc road racing world title; to a point where today American riders are accepted as masters in this branch of two wheel competition. From its insular position of the early post-Second World War days, the AMA has risen to become a vitally important part of a truly international sport.

Right
Jay Springsteen winner of the AMA National Championships in 1976, '77 and '78. He was at his best on the spectacular flat tracks so popular in the States

Castrol

XR
750

Freddie Spencer during his early days on a Honda four-stroke in AMA Superbike racing, circa 1980. Freddie went on to become the first American double World Champion in a single season (for 250 and 500 cc in 1985)

1966 Bart Markel
1967 Gary Nixon
1968 Gary Nixon
1969 Mert Lawwill
1970 Gene Romero
1971 Dick Mann
1972 Mark Brelsford
1973 Kenny Roberts
1974 Kenny Roberts
1975 Gary Scott
1976 Jay Springsteen
1977 Jay Springsteen
1978 Jay Springsteen
1979 Steve Eklund
1980 Randy Goss

It should be noted that up to and including 1953 the AMA national title was awarded on a single race, the Springfield Mile. Thereafter riders competed in a series of differing events and forms of racing to decide who would wear the coveted Number One plate the following season.

8
Bonneville Salt Flats

Bonneville is a name known throughout the motorcycling world as one synonymous with record breaking. It is not the name of a town or city, but a bed of rock-hard flat salt on the Nevada-Utah border. The seemingly endless horizon of salt 'pavement' absolutely devoid of vegetation is difficult for the stranger to comprehend.

The legendary British speedster, Noel Pope (shown here in England) took his supercharged v-twin JAP powered Brough Superior to Bonneville in 1949, but a series of disasters – including a crash at around 150 mph – saw his attempts to set a new World Speed Record come to nothing

Millions of years ago, the entire western area of North America from California to the Rocky mountains, lay at the bottom of carboniferous seas. The shrinking and shifting of the planet during the Miocene period raised the land from below the ocean to an altitude of many thousands of feet above it. It was during that process that the limestone beds of this sea floor were thrown upward and dropped, until the area of land that was Western America consisted of a chaotic mix of mountains and valleys. But within a very short time after the mountains were thrust upwards, the forces of erosion began their battle to wear and tear them asunder, which ultimately left the landscape of weather-worn crags – with some

Throughout the 1950s the American Hot Rod Association and others held speed sessions at Bonneville. Machinery was varied and included Vincents, Triumphs, Indians and Harley-Davidsons – one of the latter is illustrated

mountains high and mighty, whilst others are little more than hillocks.

However, in the area which was to finally emerge as the state of Utah, a different situation was created – a basin with no outlet. Towards the end of the ice age (some 100,000 years ago), when the Utah climate was wet and cold, small glaciers flowed down from the highest peaks, forming a huge lake. This was Lake Bonneville and, although it is now virtually non-existent, the salt basin still bears its name. Lake Bonneville once covered an area measuring 100 × 200 miles; today the Bonneville salt flats are 15 miles long and eight miles wide.

To fully appreciate the vast expanse of the original lake, one has to realise that both Wendover and Salt Lake City, 100 miles apart on opposite shores, rest upon its base. The lake water at one time reached a full 1,000 feet above the present site of both these towns!

What process brought about today's situation? Briefly, the giant lake was reduced to a glistening bed of salt by one simple process – evaporation. More water evaporated than flowed in, and the water became more and more saline until it became the crust that it is today.

Contrary to popular belief, the Bonneville salt flats are not dry all the year round, in fact during the winter months the surface is usually covered with a few inches of water, caused by heavy rainfall. Consequently the most suitable time of year for would-be record breakers is in late August or early September, when the salt flats are at their driest.

After the Second World War Bonneville became the centre for the record-breaking fraternity. This was for two reasons; the recent political upheavals caused by the conflict, and with speeds rising it was becoming even harder to find a suitable venue within the European borders.

In 1949 the legendary British speedster, Noel Pope, took his blown v-twin JAP powered Brough Superior to Bonneville. Theoretically his fully streamlined machine should have been capable of over 200 mph, but a series of disasters – including a crash at around 150 mph – saw him get nowhere near this figure before the machine was damaged beyond repair, forcing Pope to retreat back across the Atlantic to lick his wounds.

American Rollie Free stole much of the limelight at Bonneville during the immediate post-war years. Riding a 998 cc Vincent Black Lightning v-twin he established several AMA records over a five year period, between 1950 and 1955. During this time several other riders challenged him for honours. Usually mounted on Harley-Davidson or Triumph machines, these included Joe Simpson, Bus Schaller, Bobby Kelton and Bud Hare.

The AMA sanctioned two distinct classes: A and C. The latter was limited to semi-stock bikes using only the manufacturers' catalogued parts and running on petrol, with compression ratios limited to 8:1 and no supercharging. For class A, although supercharging was not permitted, there was no limitation on fuel or technical modifications.

By the end of 1954 the major American National

Right
View of the Harley v-twin engine. Note massive Italian Dell'Orto carbs, duplex primary chain and small peanut fuel tank on this example

Below
In the early 1960s Don Vesco achieved a two-way average of 126.93 mph on this Manx Norton with no special tuning. Fairing shows the scars of an earlier fall

Above

The nearest town to the Bonneville Salt Flat, Utah is Salt Lake City – a view from 1956

Left

The German NSU company undertook a series of record breaking attempts in August 1956; machinery included this 250 Rennmax racing twin

Records achieved at Bonneville stood as follows: Class C fastest M Dickerson (Vincent) 147.58 mph 6 September 1953; 1,200 cc F Ludlow (Indian) 120.74 mph 25 September 1938. Class A fastest R Free (Vincent) 160.73 mph 10 September 1953; 1,200 cc R Kucera (Harley-Davidson) 139.49 mph 5 September 1953.

Meanwhile the absolute world motorcycle speed record had been upped by New Zealander, Russell Wright riding yet another Vincent at Swannanoa, New Zealand on 2 July 1955 to 185 mph. This followed the German Wilhelm Herz who had reached 180.17 mph with a 498 cc supercharged NSU dohc twin some four years earlier on the Munich-Ingolstadt *autobahn*.

Now at last Bonneville was to come into its own. Less than a month after Wright's record a 22-year-old Texan, Johnny Allen achieved 193.72 mph with a 649 cc Triumph twin using cigar-shaped streamlining. Unfortunately for both Allen and Triumph, his run was not recognised by the sport's international body, the FIM.

However, the name Bonneville finally made it into the FIM's record books, when on 4 August 1956 Herz and NSU journeyed to the Utah salt flats to set a new world record of 210.64 mph. Just two days

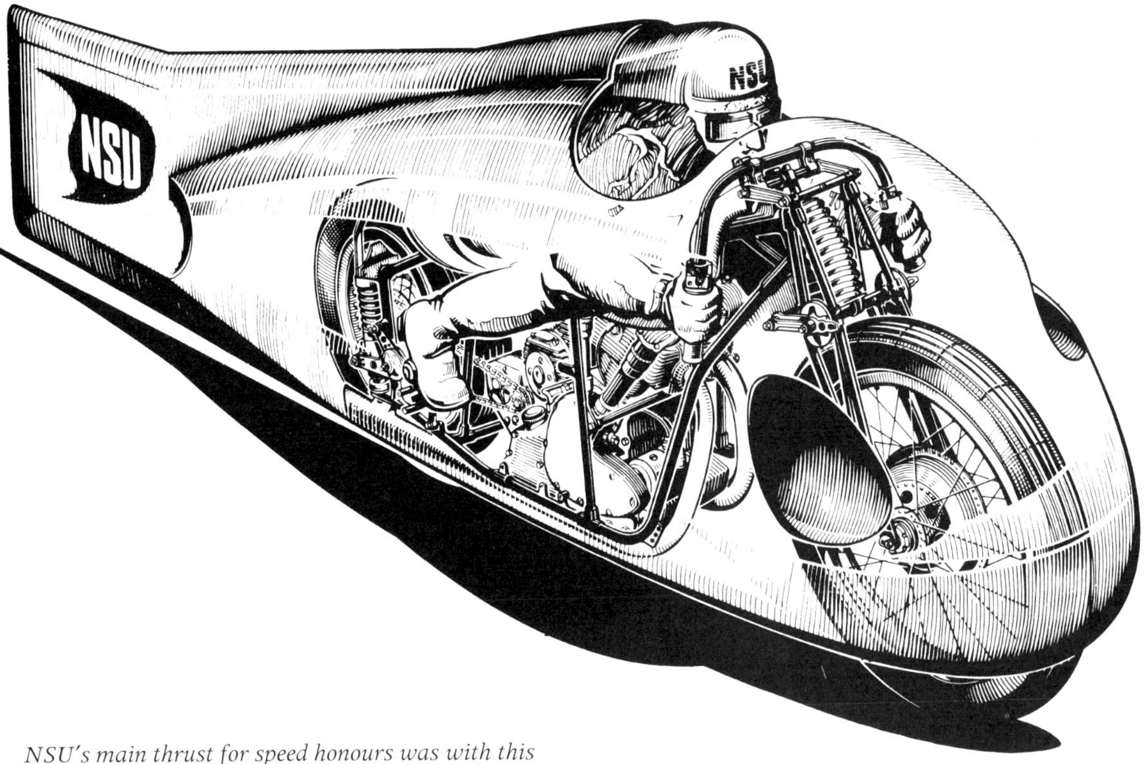

NSU's main thrust for speed honours was with this supercharged 498cc dohc twin – a modified version of the machine which had broken the record back in 1951

previously the same rider had set a new 350 cc record at over 189 mph.

After Hertz and the NSU *equipe* had departed for the return journey back to Germany, Johnny Allen staged another attempt to wrest the speed crown. He was confident that his streamlined Triumph was capable of even greater speeds than the NSU, and this he proved by achieving a two-way speed of 214 mph. But once again, the FIM was not involved in timing the runs and so it didn't become an 'official' record – even though this time the FIM took a full six months before they threw out Allen's record claim.

In 1962 Bill Johnson, a Los Angeles trucker, appeared on the salt flats with another cigar-shaped Triumph twin. This time the services of FIM-approved time keepers were secured and so when Johnson's 649 cc Triumph sped through the speed traps at a two-way average of 224.57 mph Bonneville had its first ever American world speed record. This was not quite as easy as it may have sounded as Johnson's attempt so nearly ended in disaster rather than the ultimate success it achieved when the Joe Dudek-built Triumph streamliner got into a perilous drift at around 230 mph. Next on the scene was Bob Leppan, a Detroit Triumph dealer who blasted across the salt flats in 1966 to set a new speed of 245.66 mph in a streamliner named Gyronaut XI, powered by a pair of six-fifty Triumph engines.

As a way of extra publicity Harley-Davidson began to take an active interest in Bonneville. Their first attempts were with a specially prepared short-stroke 248 cc Aermacchi road racing engine enclosed in a 14 ft long alloy shell. Ridden by works rider Roger Reiman this device averaged 156.24 mph for the flying mile and 156.54 mph for the kilometre in 1964. The records were approved by the AMA but not the FIM as no recognised observer was present from the latter organisation. Hence the speeds constituted American records only. However Harley achieved its ambition the following year when George Roeder piloted a revised version of the sprint streamliner to a new world speed record at the breathtaking speed of 177.225 mph – sanctioned by the FIM.

In late September 1970 the Milwaukee factory made its first really serious bid for the outright motorcycle world speed record. This came only a few days after Don Vesco had bettered Leppan's record by almost 4 mph with a double engined Yamaha two-stroke on 17 September (the engines were 348 cc TR2 racing units). Ripping through the Bonneville timing lights at a two-way average of

255.37 mph for the flying mile, leading AMA road racer Cal Rayborn captured the record for Harley-Davidson.

Next day, Rayborn tried to hoist the record still higher. But, after clocking over 260 mph one way, his engine blew on the return run. The record-breaker was powered by a v-twin engine the capacity of which had been increased to 1480 cc. Pump petrol was used.

A few short days later first Vesco and then Leppan attempted to retrieve their respective Bonneville world speed crowns. Vesco couldn't match the Harley figure, while Leppan, now with two 750 cc Triumph engines instead of coupled six-fifties, somersaulted end over end at 260 mph after the front suspension failed. Leppan was seriously injured in the ensuing accident, so putting a stop to his challenge.

Despite repeated attacks the following year Rayborn's record still stood at the end of the 1971 Bonneville Speed Week, which saw a record number of machines taking part. The most spectacular of these attempts was that undertaken by a fantastic 900 lb eight cylinder twin engined 1500 cc Honda called the Hawk, piloted by Jon McKibben. However, after a one-way 286.567 mph he crashed the 21 ft long projectile while travelling at around 270 mph – fortunately without serious injury. Amazing considering that McKibben's machine slid $1\frac{1}{2}$ miles on its side! Don Vesco had the satisfaction of setting a new 250 cc world record in the same week with a streamliner powered by a 250 cc Yamaha engine, his two-way average was 172.455 mph.

Mechanics ready the Delphin III for its successful record attempt

Above

The 1956 NSU Delphin III with which Wilhelm Herz set a new world speed record of 210.64 mph at Bonneville Salt Flats on 4 August 1956

Right

Roger Rieman achieved an average speed of 156.24 mph for the flying mile at Bonneville in 1964 on this 246 cc Aermacchi HD Sprint powered streamliner. The new 250 cc record was approved by the AMA, but not the FIM; so it remained an American only achievement

Two years later a Norton powered 1,700 cc double-engined machine appeared at Bonneville with drag racing specialist Boris Murray cocooned in the comprehensive streamliner. This achieved over 260 mph, but again could only manage it one-way – so Rayborn's record remained. In another attempt

NSU
NSU
NSU
DELPHIN III

SPRINT
GOODYEAR
HARLEY-DAVIDSON

Above
Cal Rayborn's 1480cc Harley-Davidson v-twin engined streamliner as used in successful world record attempt (265.49 mph) at Bonneville, October 1970

Below
Harley-Davidson team and machine, for Rayborn's October 1970 record attempt. The rider (pilot!) is third from the right

Rayborn setting out on his two way run which was to culminate in a new speed record and a place in the history books

View of Bonneville Salt Flats gives an idea of the terrain faced by would-be record breakers. This photograph was taken in September 1977

the following year the Norton streamliner blew itself to pieces.

Then in October 1974 Californian Don Vesco returned to Bonneville on a twin-engined red and yellow streamliner called the 'Silver Bird'. Using a pair of Yamaha TZ700 four cylinder two-stroke racing engines, Vesco set an incredible average of 281.7 mph, reaching 287.5 mph on his second run. However, he was later excluded as he had changed the rubber drive belts linking the two engines between runs which he later found out to his cost was against the rules.

Undaunted, Vesco by now 36 years old, returned to the Bonneville salt flats on 28 September 1975 with the same Yamaha, but now equipped with breaking parachutes. Even a 275 mph crash when 'Silver Bird' was blown off course failed to dent Vesco's ambition and after repairs he went out to achieve not only a new world speed record, but the first to top the magic 300 mark – 302.92 mph!

Not content to rest on his laurels, Vesco returned yet again to Bonneville on 25 August 1978 with the streamliner. It was now equipped with a pair of four cylinder dohc 1,000 cc Kawasaki engines, which in turbocharged mode pumped out an impressive 250 bhp, giving Vesco the power to break his own record, with a new speed of 314.355 mph. A mere three days later and Vesco increased this to 318.598 mph – achieving 323 mph through the final $\frac{1}{4}$ mile of his first run.

Others might come later, but the Bonneville salt flats of the late 1970s belonged to one man, Don Vesco – a true American hero of motorcycle sport.

9

Daytona International Speedway

Bill France Senior is very much 'Mr Daytona'. It was he who was the driving force behind bringing the famous '200' to Daytona in the first place, and he also provided the legendary event with its permanent home, the Daytona International Speedway complex. The France family has obviously done well out of this, but deservedly so; without them 'Daytona – The World Centre of Racing' would not exist.

Bill France moved to the Daytona area in 1934; the following year he witnessed that great ultimate speed seeker, Sir Malcolm Campbell make his land speed record run, the last man to gain the 'world's fastest' crown on the beach at Daytona.

France Snr. first became a motor sport promoter in 1938 – running both motorcycle and stock car races on the Daytona Beach; but these events were not without their problems. Noise, population growth, crowd control, accidents – all caused headaches to France and his team. And although his events on both two and four wheels gained in stature Bill France could visualise the day when racing on the beach would be unacceptable. So, in 1953, he began planning the ultimate solution: a purpose built circuit complex in the Daytona Beach area. But this in itself was no easy task and the transition from dream to reality took six long years. But there was to be a happy ending: the creation and opening of the Daytona International Speedway.

The new venue's first event was not concerned with bikes, being the Daytona 500 stock car race.

The first Daytona 200 to take place in the confines of the new International Speedway complex was the 1961 event. Here a BSA Gold Star competitor (2) leads with a Triumph pushing hard through the infield section

Above
A pair of BSA Gold Star riders fighting their own battle during the 1961 Daytona 200 miler

Left
Harley-Davidson teamster, Roger Reiman, winner of the first Daytona '200' to be staged at the International Speedway circuit, March 1961

Right
A section of the Daytona International Speedway complex, 'The World Centre of Racing'

The year was 1959. With its successful adoption by the four wheel brigade it may seem strange that the first motorcycle meeting was not staged until February 1961. This was not held under AMA rules, but instead was the first FIM approved road race ever staged in the USA – a full report of which appears in Chapter 7.

The first AMA sanctioned event – the 24th annual AMA National Championship – was the 200 mile Experts race, run for many years previously on an oval comprising a two mile stretch of beach linked by two sweeping turns to a back leg of tarmac. Riding a Harley-Davidson KR 750 cc side valve v-twin, 22 year old Roger Reiman scored a convincing win in 2 hours, 53 minutes, 17.15 seconds at an average

DAYTONA SPEEDWAY
DAYTONA·USA
3

Competitors round a turn in front of the massed grandstand area during the mid 1960s

speed of 69.25 mph for the 200 mile, 100 lap race. From the second lap onwards Reiman defied all challengers at the head of the field – helped in no small part by the thought of the $2,500 (£950 at the prevailing exchange rate) first prize.

In addition to his scheduled fuel stop Reiman pulled in to his pit again later just to check the fuel level but was off again in five seconds. At the finish he was 40 seconds ahead of the runner up, Don Burnett on a 490 cc Triumph twin. Third was George Roeder on another 750 KR Harley. Reiman's victory was sweet consolation for the previous years' '200' disappointment when he finished 18th after running out of fuel, and was the seventh win in succession for the Harley-Davidson factory.

The new Daytona Speedway complex was available for use in almost any branch of motorised events from motorcycles to sports cars, Formula junior stock cars and even drag racing. The facilities available were second to none at the time. There was covered pit accommodation and ample workshop space. All the leading plug, fuel and tyre companies had permanent sites and equipment installations.

There were five basic circuits. The outer banked course was 2.5 miles in length; others that took in artificial bends and straights across the infield varied from 1.63, 1.66, 3.1 and 3.81 miles – plus a number of variations, one of which was used by the AMA for the 1961 200 miler.

The infield which included a 45-acre lake suitable for speed boat racing could accommodate upwards of 65,000 spectators and their cars. The six grandstands, one of which was covered and held 6,500,

cafeteria for the competitors ensured that the 'inner man' was taken care of from dawn to dusk.

The whole complex covered 446 acres next to Highway 92, the main carriageway between Daytona Beach and all points West and North. The imposing entrance even had its own main office block, press reception and fuelling station. All were in constant, instant contact with any part of the track and all the control points by telephone.

One of the reasons why it took almost two years from the first stock car meeting in 1959 until motorcycle racing began in 1961 was that the AMA Competition Committee initially had reservations about the safety of racing bikes on the 33 degree steep banked turns on a certain section of the circuit. Finally a compromise was reached between the AMA officials and the pairing of Bill France and the amenable mayor of Daytona Beach, in which motorcycles would be restricted to a 2-mile road course in the infield portion of the race track only.

1962 was to prove something of a vintage year for the '200'. The race was led in the early stages by that great American rider Carroll Resweber, but after 21 laps the Harley rider had his engine blow in a big way. The next leader was another all time favourite, Joe Leonard, but he too was soon forced into early retirement.

catered for 35,000 people. The Press facilities were truly first class and the public address system ensured that everyone could hear the announcements at all times. The hospital in the infield could cope with most emergencies.

On the infield too was the box-tower scoreboard called 'Times Square' which could be seen from all areas of the complex. Illuminated 'telesigns' spelt out confirmed positions and times. The lap scoring and time keeping box had a photo-finish camera. A

Right
The 1966 Daytona 200 winner Buddy Elmore taking the flag after finishing second the following year

Overleaf
Triumph works rider Buddy Elmore during the 1967 Daytona 200

Daytona March 1967. One of the specially prepared Bob Hanson Honda CB450 racers. Riders were 'Swede' Savage and Harry Schaffer. But they couldn't match the Triumph or Harley-Davidson effort

From then on in there were only two men who could win – Dick Mann riding a Matchless G50 ohc single and the previous years' second finisher, Triumph-mounted Don Burnett. Mann's bike was obviously quicker, but the result finally went to the Triumph rider after Mann had stalled his engine after taking on fuel. The finish margin between the two combatants was a mere ten feet – the closest finish ever seen in a 200 miler.

The next three men home were all on Harley KRs: Ralph White, Roger Reiman and Sid Payne. In fact 13 of the first 20 home were riding the Milwaukee v-twins. Burnett's time was 2 hours, 46 minutes, 55 seconds a speed of 71.98 mph – over $2\frac{1}{2}$ mph faster than 1961.

In 1963 the motorcycles were allowed streamlining for the first time in the Daytona classic. This rule not only assisted maximum speeds, but also forced the riders to adopt a European riding style. Yet it was not the use of fairings which created the headlines, rather the controversy which surrounded the use by some riders – including Dick Mann – of the Matchless G50. AMA rules said that 50 had to be sold in a production street version. Matchless had complied by creating the G50 CSR roadster, but this bike didn't use the road racers frame; instead it used a road type as fitted to the standard production ohv singles and twins. The AMA banned the bike from Daytona! This created a furore over similar lines to that experienced a decade earlier when the Featherbed-framed Manx Norton had been banned in the early 1950s.

The pro-American competitors were pleased, those supporting a more open approach accused the AMA of more rule bending; Harley-Davidson just sat and laughed it out ... and went on to gain another victory. This win came via Ralph White who had taken his KR side valver round fastest in practice at 78.80 mph. His race average speed was to be 77.7 mph. White was the only rider to complete the full 100 lap race distance.

Reiman was back on winning form to take the 1964 event, held for the first time over the 3.81 mile

Another 1967 shot – number 9 is Gary Nixon's race winning Triumph; number 53 KR750 Harley-Davidson

Two Harley's and a BSA A50 twin taking on fuel during Daytona practice 1967. Number 25 is Cal Rayborn with the Andres-tuned KR750

circuit which utilised the steep 33 degree turns – the AMA having at last relented on the earlier ban. Reiman (Harley KR) rode a controlled, professional race eventually pulling clear of his rivals to take his second '200' victory.

The following year there was a new hazard, one many of the competitors had never encountered before – rain! Winner Reiman and second placed man Mert Lawwill made it all look incredibly easy; whilst others slipped and slid, the two works Harley stars circulated in a fast, safe manner; Reiman's average of 90.04 mph a lasting testament of their progress in exceedingly difficult weather conditions.

The years 1966 and 1967 saw a massive reversal of fortunes for the Harley-Davidson team, with British Triumph twins largely dominating the proceedings. Buddy Elmore (1966) and Gary Nixon (1967) winning at average speeds of 96.58 and 98.22 mph respectively. The nearest a Harley man got to victory in those two years was George Roeder with a second place in 1966 and third in 1967.

It was Triumph's turn to be upstaged in 1968 when Harley-Davidson and Yamaha were the leading bikes. Although Cal Rayborn won on a Harley, this year was really the first truly *international* Daytona '200', with the likes of Mike Duff and Yvon Du Hamel (Canada), Phil Read, Peter Williams and Rod Gould (Britain) and Mitsuo Otoh (Japan) all in the line up. The most successful of these foreign riders was Du Hamel who brought his four-speed prototype 350 TR2 Yamaha home in second place, but a lap adrift to Rayborn. (AMA rules at that time restricted the number of gears to a maximum of four).

So why had Harley-Davidson suddenly come back on song? Well, much of this is explained in Chapter 4, but suffice to say that race chief Dick O'Brien and his loyal crewmen had been burning the midnight oil in an attempt to recreate their venerable side valve KR racer into a machine capable of winning races in the late 1960s. And, as Rayborn's victory shows, they were successful too, the 1968 bikes bearing little resemblance to the machines which had been blown into the weeds over the previous two seasons.

Right from the initial days of practice it was evident that the Harley technicians had done their home work correctly. In all, there were seven factory entries in the 1968 200 miler: Cal Rayborn, Roger Reiman, Mert Lawwill, Bart Markel, Fred Nix, Walt Fulton Jnr and Dan Haaby.

Rayborn's winning average speed of 101.29 mph was over 3 mph quicker than Nixon's Triumph win of a year earlier, effectively meaning that the 490 cc pushrod Triumph twins were no longer in the hunt;

Above
Robert Vintners (21) from Fort Smith, Arkansas, BSA team rider. Although he was destined to retire from the '200', Vintners finished 3rd in the 250 cc race as a member of the Yamaha team, March 1967

Right
Practice 1967; Triumph pit line-up

Overleaf
Triumph teammates Gary Nixon (9) and Dick Hammer (16) enter the infield roads from banked oval section of Daytona International Speedway, 19 March 1967

their leading rider Buddy Elmore finishing in 6th place, 2 laps behind Rayborn.

If Triumph were no longer a threat, the same couldn't be said of Yamaha, with not only Du Hamel in runner up position but also Art Baumann finishing third on one of the ultra rapid 350 cc twins. Also Harley were lucky, really lucky . . . Rayborn was the only survivor from the seven man team!

1969 and Rayborn set the seal on his claim to be America's leading road racer of the era when he won again at Daytona. This time opposition came not only from Yamaha, but also Suzuki in the shape of Ron Grant (2nd) with Yamaha-mounted Duff third.

Although Rayborn was to show further touches of brilliance in future years, Harley was never again to win the coveted Daytona 200 miler. In fact, except for Dick Mann's 1971 BSA victory, every year since has seen a Japanese bike on the winners rostrum. But this state of affairs has not meant less exciting racing, far from it! First came 1970 and a truly titanic battle between the Japanese factories and the by then financially stricken British BSA/Triumph empire.

The backdrop to the 1970 Daytona 200 was the AMA decision to scrap the rules limiting all four-stroke engines (except side valve 750s!) to a maximum capacity of 500 cc. Instead all manufacturers were allowed to race 750 cc motorcycles regardless of valve type. There is no doubt in the author's mind that this rule change was responsible more than any

RACING
TRIUMPH
TEAM
TRIUMPH
3

other event for road racing becoming popular throughout thc Statcs.

Cycle World called it the 'Battle of the Giants' and so it was, with the British, Japanese and American factories meeting in a head on confrontation for honours. The supporting races comprised a 250 cc event for both experts and amateurs alike (which for 1970 saw 350 cc four-strokes allowed for the first time). This turned out to be a Yamaha benefit, even though Harley-Davidson had one of the latest 350 Aermacchi horizontal singles flown over from Italy specially for its top rider, Cal Rayborn. However, much to the Milwaukee factory's disappointment it was some ten miles an hour slower than the Yamahas. The race was won by Australian Kel Carruthers, the 1969 250 cc World Champion, who proved to everyone willing to admit what they saw, just why he won the world title. Within two laps Kel had the lead and the only person who could stay anywhere near him was Englishman Rod Gould, one of Kel's closest competitors in Europe. The bike Carruthers rode was entered and tuned by the Californian Don Vesco. After Daytona Vesco went on to become the fastest man on two wheels with his twin engines Yamaha device, whilst Carruthers settled in the USA and later was the man behind Kenny Roberts' rise to the top.

With Carruthers and Gould finishing 1st and 2nd, 3rd place went to Yvon Du Hamel, riding for Trevor Deeley, the Canadian Yamaha importer. So for the first time in the history of the 100 mile '250' race not one American rider was represented in the winners circle.

The 100 mile Amateur race was won by Rusty

Above
Four Yamahas complete the first lap of the 1967 250cc event with race winner Gary Nixon leading, followed by Mike Duff (10), Robert Vinters (21) and Donald Twigg (31)

Left
Nixon waves after his winning ride in the 1967 Daytona '200'

Bradley who took over the lead as early as the first lap and never relinquished it. Rusty qualified his three cylinder 500 cc Kawasaki two-stroke faster than any other Kawasaki, regardless of whether it was ridden by an expert or an amateur (which produced a crop of red faces from certain professional riders!). His average speed of 100.72 mph broke the amateur record set the previous year by over four miles an hour.

But the race everyone was waiting to see was the 200 miler; every one looked a winner – except the combination which won. In practice BSA and Triumph were running faster than anyone else on their super sounding three cylinder racers. With special frames, five-speed boxes and almost more horsepower than they knew what to do with, they looked strong.

Suzuki were a dark horse with their TR500 two-stroke twins. They had won the last National of 1969 and everyone knew that they had done quite a bit of development work through the winter. With Jody Nicholas, Ron Grant, Art Baumann and Jim Odom in the saddles, Suzuki were looking powerful.

Harley-Davidson didn't look like winners after qualifying with their best bike ten miles an hour down on Gene Romero's new record qualifying time of 157.34 mph on one of the Triumph Tridents. Harley's best, Bart Markel only managed a shade over 147 mph, whilst their star rider, Cal Rayborn, was two miles an hour slower.

In the Yamaha garage there was a quiet air of optimism. They had two machines, ridden by Kel Carruthers and Rod Gould, in the top ten qualifiers and they were sure that these two would be around at the end of 200 miles.

Kawasaki were a little worried. Their fastest bike had won the amateur race and they didn't really know how they'd do in the big one.

And last, but certainly not least, was Honda. They had some good riders; Ralph Bryans and Tommy Robb, both Grand Prix stars from Ireland. And they had that old man whom everyone always seemed to forget, Mr Cool himself, Dick Mann, 17 years on the National trail. Dick qualified at 152.67 mph and looked like he'd be in the hunt except for the fact that all week Honda had been troubled by oiling and cam chain problems. After watching the Hondas in practice, puffing smoke with every downshift, no one expected them to last the distance.

So came the day of the race with BSA and Triumph looking sure fire winners and Yamaha and Harley as pretty safe bets for getting on to the leader board.

When the flag dropped Dick Mann stole a lead over everyone else and got to the banking first, but during that first circuit of the oval Gary Nixon, on a Triumph and Mike Hailwood, second fastest qualifier on a BSA, passed Mann. As the riders headed into the infield it was Nixon, Hailwood, Mann and then a group consisting of Rayborn, Grant, Carruthers, Gould and then everybody else. On that first infield lap two possible winners were

knocked out of contention. An unidentified rider torpedoed Art Baumann's Suzuki causing it to collide with Ralph White's Yamaha and they both went down, Art with a dislocated arm and Ralph with a broken ankle. Two laps later Andy Lascoutx squeezed his throttle a shade too much coming out of a turn and took Rod Gould with him ... both ended up in hospital.

Three laps later Mike Hailwood was out with a holed piston – just the first of the BSAs and Triumphs to have a problem. In practice the factory mechanics had discovered that at high revs the

Left
Cal Rayborn with the winners trophy after the 1968 Daytona '200'

Below
Rayborn pictured with the final variant of the long-running Harley-Davidson KR750, Daytona March 1969

points were bouncing, causing a pre-ignition problem. Even though this was found out in practice it was too late to do something about it so they had to let it go. Consequently Hailwood and Nixon both dropped out because of it. Other factory BSAs and Triumphs had a mis-firing problem but at least it didn't drop them out of the hunt.

By now the race had settled down to a battle between Gary Nixon, whose bike hadn't broken yet, Ron Grant, on his Suzuki, Dick Mann and just a little

Right
Ron Grant the English born Suzuki works rider was runner-up in 1969 behind Rayborn

Below
Although Dick Mann and Honda eventually won the 1970 Daytona 200 it was the BSA and Triumph triples which were clearly the fastest bikes that year. This is Don Castro's Triumph – he finished 3rd

astern, Cal Rayborn and Kel Carruthers. The duelling was fast and furious.

Many knowledgeable observers, before the race began, were predicting that there would be quite a race to the 100 mile mark but that most of the fancied riders wouldn't be around at the finish. How true this was. At, or around 100 mile mark frontrunners began to drop by the wayside. Ron Grant ran low on fuel, so low that his engine started to run lean and

That wily old fox Dick Mann gained another victory (and more kisses!) in 1971, this time he did it on a BSA

Right
Cal Rayborn (left) and Kel Carruthers after their success in the 250 cc race, on Vesco Yamahas at Daytona in 1971. Also in picture is Kel's wife Jan and children Sharon and Paul

CARRUTHERS
YAMAHA
DUANE
YAMAHA
TWIN 'K' SPORT CENTER
KONI

BATES
10

Above
Dave Aldana BSA team member in 1970 and 1971

Left
Aldana also undertook record breaking with a Yoshimura tuned Kawasaki Z1 900cc roadster at Daytona in 1971

Right
The talented Art Baumann, the nearest he came to winning the '200' was in 1968 with a 3rd. However, he could have won in 1973 and 1974 if his Kawasakis had stayed together

Overleaf
Baumann (Kawasaki 71) leads a couple of Yamahas

consequently seized. At just over 100 miles Nixon lost his engine. Tom Rockwood was running sixth at the midway point but his bike wouldn't start after his pit stop. Cal Rayborn lost a piston as did team mate Bart Markel later on.

While all this was going on people further back started to make their move. Gene Romero, who had run out of brakes on lap two and overshot a corner, was slowly making his way back through the traffic. Don Castro, on a works Triumph, was also quietly getting his job done and by now was running in the top six.

Because of the high expected speeds for the 1970 event there was a new type of starting system used for all the Daytona events that year. The 30 fastest qualifiers left at the first flag, five seconds later the next 30 went and five seconds after that the last 30 or so started.

In this last 30, because of qualifying difficulties were Tommy Robb and Yvon Du Hamel. Needless to say they started to carve their way through the pack from the first lap on. Tommy dropped out early due to machine troubles but Du Hamel kept going. By the fifteenth circuit he was running in tenth spot and he continued his upward climb to the very end. Finishing in fourth place, Yvon impressed many as being probably the fastest rider on the course, Mike Hailwood notwithstanding. The only other men that seemed to be in his class were Kel Carruthers, Rod Gould, Ron Grant and Gary Nixon.

So the race ended with the winning Mann and machine that everybody forgot about. Dick Mann won and he deserved it. He rode a supremely well-judged race and never made a mistake. Following him home came the two Triumphs ridden by Romero and Castro. Fourth was Du Hamel, just pipping New Zealands Geoff Parry. Next came the first Harley to finish which was piloted by Walt Fulton Jr. Interestingly Walt bypassed the new XR overhead valve model (as used by Rayborn and Markel) for the older

19

71
111

Right
Art Baumann with the fire breathing Kawasaki H2R 750 two-stroke triple at Daytona in 1973 – fast but fragile. Of the six examples entered all were doomed to retire that year

Below
Gary Nixon (Kawasaki) leads Alex George (Suzuki) during the 1976 200-miler, Nixon finished 2nd, George 14th

Overleaf
Nixon with the mighty Kawasaki 750 Daytona. Its 748cc three cylinder two-stroke engine produced 115 bhp and a maximum speed of around 185 mph

Yamaha were to continue their winning streak for another *twelve* years until 1985 when Freddie Spencer won on a Honda. After 1979 the AMA motorcycle type rating was changed from Class C to Formula 1. The circuit length was increased first to 3.84 miles in 1973 and then to 3.87 miles from 1976 onwards.

Above
Daytona banking in 1973 – steeper than it looks!

KR side valver. The wisdom of this shows when you realise that the next Harley was way down the field in eighteenth place.

So Daytona had come and gone for another year. Some new heroes were made and some old ones probably wished they'd stayed at home – all except one. For the record, Dick Mann's winning time was 1 hour, 57 minutes, 13 seconds, an average speed of 102.69 mph.

The following year, 1971, Mann was back on the winner's rostrum, this time riding a revised BSA Rocket Three. In fact the first three finishers were all mounted on either BSA or Triumph triples; the Brits having sorted out the previous year's problems. Mann averaged 104.73 mph to prove that the BSA was considerably quicker than the specially prepared works Honda CB750 he had used in 1970.

Don Emde who had finished third on a BSA in 1971 was the 1972 winner on a 350 cc Yamaha TR2B, but at the slower average speed of 103.35 mph; after most of the more fancied runners had dropped by the wayside. (Don Emde and his father have the distinction of being the only father and son combination to have both been winners of the Daytona 200). Multi world champion Phil Read brought his ageing 750 Norton home in fourth place.

Kawasaki
30
Castrol
RENOLD

333

GOODYEAR
BELL

Left
Canadian Kawasaki star, Yvon Du Hamel

Below
A young (and deadly serious!) Eddie Lawson with the Moriwaki Kawasaki four cylinder four-stroke he raced in the 1980 Daytona '200'. He first rode in the event in 1979 on a Yamaha, finishing 33rd. He went on to become a Daytona winner and multi world champion

Right
Freddie Spencer (right) and Roberto Pietri in the 1981 Daytona Superbike race. Both are Honda mounted

There were some famous winners too: Jarno Saarinen (1973), Giacomo Agostini (1974), Gene Romero (1975), Johnny Cecotto (1976), Steve Baker (1977), Kenny Roberts (1978), Dale Singleton (1979) and Patrick Pons (1980).

By the end of the 1970s the Daytona 200 had become the most important road race in the world; a fitting tribute not only to the growth of motorcycle racing in the USA, but also to the foresight of men such as Bill France, the 'father' of the Daytona races.

10
Transatlantic

American riders (and sometimes motorcycles) have often crossed the Atlantic Ocean to compete in Europe down through the years. As revealed in Chapter 1 this began almost as soon as the motorcycle went racing at the turn of the century. In the immediate post Second World War period these forays were usually limited to the Isle of Man, where riders such as Nick Nicholson, Ed 'La Belle and John Marcote appeared in the TT series during the 1950s.

Then during the 1960s a fresh set of faces appeared on the European scene including Frank Scuria, Jess Thomas and Lance Weil. But the really big event was the birth of the Anglo-American Match Races in early 1971.

First details of the new series were released in February 1971 when the press on both sides of the Atlantic carried the story that a three-day 'festival of speed' would take place over the Easter weekend. The venues would be Brands Hatch, Mallory Park and Oulton Park. The driving force behind the idea came from two men: Chris Lowe of Motor Circuit Developments (owners of the three circuits involved) and Peter Deverall, President of the American BSA organisation. Journalists called it potentially 'the greatest and most fiercely contested road

During the 1950s several American riders crossed the Atlantic to race in the Isle of Man, including Nick Nicholson (Manx Norton), seen here in the 1953 Senior TT

race competition since the world championship hey-day of 500 MV versus 500 Honda and 250 Honda versus 250 Yamaha'.

Later the same month it was revealed that all the riders would be mounted on BSA or Triumph 3-cylinder models – as raced at Daytona and other circuits by factory riders over the preceding months; Gene Romero would head the American team which would also include Dick Mann, Jim Rice and Don Castro.

At first glance, the British team of Ray Pickrell, John Cooper, Paul Smart, Percy Tait and Tony Jefferies seemed unbeatable with their home track advantage and the fact that they were expert short circuit racers, whereas the Americans had only Dick Mann as a really experienced road racer, the others being essentially dirt, rather than tarmac riders. The Stateside team was further weakened by the absence of their most experienced tarmac star in the shape of Gary Nixon who had been sidelined with a broken leg. Finally, not only was the American team selection restricted to riders under contract to BSA or Triumph, but their bikes were in AMA-race trim with big seats and tanks. By contrast the British teamsters had 'slimline' short circuit small tanks and seats. In spite of all the odds stacked against them, the Americans put up a truly splendid fight and it

Overleaf
Dave Aldana (BSA Rocket Three) at Oulton Park, Easter Monday 1971

Lance Weil in action on his Cycle World *sponsored 883 cc ohv Harley-Davidson during the Hutchinson 100, Brands Hatch, 13 August 1967*

American Lance Weil created a lot of media attention when he raced on the British short circuits in 1967

Castrol
AMAL

The first ever Anglo-American Match Race Series was run over Easter 1971. Here's the American team, left to right: Don Castro, Gary Nixon, Jim Rice, Dave Aldana, Dick Mann and Don Emde

quickly became apparent that the Transatlantic match race series was a winner.

The initial clash of the two wheeled titans took place at Brands Hatch, a tight demanding circuit some 20 miles south east of the English capital. Britain's Ray Pickrell was in outstanding form, snapping up both heats and setting a new circuit lap record in the process. At the end of that first day, the points were added up and Britain led 69–49. America's top rider, as expected, was Dick Mann who scored one third and one fourth to become the USA's top points scorer.

The next day saw the riders travel to Mallory Park, another of the tight British short circuits. Whilst Pickrell continued on his winnning way, Mann again upheld American honour with a third place. Although Britain won at Mallory by 53–48, the score had a mere five point difference because, although the British riders were filling the top two positions, the Americans were piling up points for packing the mid field placings. At the final venue, Oulton Park, the Americans could not repeat this and went down 69–40; Britain taking the series 183–137.

The first Transatlantic Match Races proved an unqualified success. Not only had it roused considerable interest in the motorcycling press in both America and Britain, but well over 50,000 spectators had paid to watch the teams do battle. All this paved the way for a major sponsorship deal by the John Player cigarette company for the 1972 series, and so the event became known as the John Player Transatlantic Trophy Challenge.

By this time, however, the BSA-Triumph group was in serious financial difficulties and so the Americans were at last able to compete on other makes of bikes. This meant that the USA could select and field a much more powerful team, particularly as this included America's top road racer, Cal Rayborn on an XR750 Harley-Davidson v-twin. The '72 team comprised Rayborn, Mann, Don Emde, Jody Nicolas, Ron Grant and Art Baumann.

The superior team selection was not confined to the American effort, as the British now had multi world champion Phil Read, together with Peter Williams and Tony Rutter. This trio joined Pickrell, Cooper and Jefferies.

Again Brands Hatch got the proceedings under way, and in the first heat Pickrell repeated his winning action from the year before. However, the British fans and riders were in for a big shock as in heat two Rayborn, who had never raced at the Kent cir-

Right
Gary Nixon (right) with Dick Mann, Oulton Park, 1971

Below
The hero of the 1972 Easter Match races was Cal Rayborn (left) and his Harley-Davidson XR750

cuit before, or for that matter on any British track, stormed past Pickrell and held on to score a headline grabbing victory. Nobody knew it at the time, but this was to be the forerunner of the American surge to the top in road racing at world level, which was to gain speed during the remainder of the 1970s, ending with almost total domination during the following decade and up to the present day.

As for the remainder of the 1972 Transatlantic Match Races Rayborn and Pickrell were in a class of their own and duelled throughout the three days. On the second day at Mallory Park Pickrell won the first race from the flying Harley man, whilst in the second Rayborn turned the tables, just as he had done the previous day at Brands Hatch. At Oulton Park it was Rayborn who won first, but Pickrell took the second heat to square the wins at three each. Rayborn's outstanding contribution meant that although the Brits

Right
Rayborn leads Peter Williams (Norton), Brands Hatch Easter Match Races, 1973

Below
The two teams in friendly pose before the start of the 1974 Match Races – on display was some of the finest racing talent of the 1970s

still had more points, the final 255–212 scoreline was much closer than the '71 result.

The Americans had made their point, however. The hard riding Rayborn, who normally only competed in a half a dozen or so road races back home, had taken on the cream of British racing and beaten them three times out of six. Not only that, but upon arriving in Britain his Harley had not been expected to finish a race, let alone win!

Twelve months later and the 1972 American team returned, determined to avenge their two previous defeats. By this stage in the proceedings, the team numbers had grown. The USA line-up consisted of four Harley-Davidson mounted riders, Rayborn, Dave Sehl, Mert Lawwill and Gary Fisher (the latter normally a Yamaha rider had been loaned one of the big Milwaukee v-twins for the series). Besides the Harley men there was a trio of Kawasaki two-stroke triples ridden by Gary Nixon, Yvon Du Hamel (a Canadian) and Art Baumann. The balance of the squad consisted of Dave Aldana (Norton) and Ron Grant (Suzuki). The reserve rider was Cliff Carr (Kawasaki).

The 'home' team also looked exceptionally strong. Not only was the up-and-coming Barry Sheene included for the first time, but also Mick Grant, Paul Smart, Peter Williams, Dave Potter, Percy Tait, Dave Croxford, Tony Jefferies and John Cooper. The reserve was Ron Chandler.

In the first leg at Brands Hatch, Dave Potter was the surprise victor after many of the more fancied men struck trouble on a circuit made to resemble an ice rink after heavy rain. Yvon Du Hamel and the Harley-Davidson rider Dave Sehl were second and third respectively. Suddenly it looked possible for the Americans to take the trophy back to the States for the first time and they went into the second race at Brands in a confident mood.

This proved to be well founded as team leader Rayborn, the star of the previous year, took the lead and held onto it, despite being in severe pain from a damaged collarbone sustained a few weeks before.

With Yvon Du Hamel playing the supporting role in third place to perfection, the Yanks swept to an eleven point lead at the end of the first day of the 1973 series. As the British fans streamed out of the circuit on the way home they realised that their very best riders had been humbled at the very centre of British short circuit racing. So it was that the teams

Gary Nixon rode a works Suzuki during the 1974 series

assembled the next day at Mallory Park. The British bent on avenging their honour, the Americans bent on consolidating their advantage.

At the end the honours were shared with Peter Williams taking the first race on his ageing Norton twin, whilst the Canadian Kawasaki star Yvon Du Hamel scorched his three cylinder two-stroke to a fine win in the second. Britain now led by a mere two points!

Oulton Park on Easter Monday 1973 was very much the place to be for road racing fans. Could the Americans win at last, or would the British hold on to their slender lead? With over 20,000 spectators packing their way into the Cheshire circuit the scene was set for the showdown. As the riders brought their machines to the line for the first race an air of expectancy hung over the circuit. One man above all responded to this high pressure challenge and sadly for the Americans it was not one of their number, but the quietly spoken bespectacled Peter Williams on the John Player Norton twin. Williams was simply in a class of his own that day, winning both races; the second after a bad start which saw him come through from the back of the field to win.

In fact after excellent rides from Nixon and Yvon

Art Baumann with the fearsome Kawasaki 750 two-stroke triple at Brands Hatch, Easter Friday 1974

One of the top American teamsters of the 1974 Transatlantic series was Gene Romero. He is shown here at Brands Hatch on one of the ultra quick watercooled four cylinder TZ750 Yamahas

The man of the 1976 series was Steve Baker; representing America the Canadian won four of the six races

Du Hamel it was Williams alone who stopped the Americans winning the series, but it was close with only 18 points separating the teams at the end of the six gruelling races, over three circuits.

Things were even closer the following year when the 1974 series saw the Brits the winners by only 14 points; 415–401. This was the year which also saw the Transatlantic debut of the man destined to become America's first ever world 500 cc road race champion, Kenny Roberts. And 'King Kenny' was the star of the series – winning three of his six races and finishing second in the other three. This matched Rayborn's tremendous effort of two years earlier.

And so to 1975. The British were forced to field a below par team, with Phil Read not available, and Barry Sheene having broken his legs in a horrific crash at Daytona. Paul Smart was also sidelined through injury, John Cooper had retired, whilst three previous Match Race stars Peter Williams, Ray Pickrell and Tony Jefferies had all been forced into early retirements through serious accidents.

The American squad on the other hand was probably at its strongest with Kenny Roberts, Don Castro, Gene Romero, Pat Hennen, Dave Aldana, Steve

Overleaf
Pat Hennen cranks his works Suzuki RG500 over near the limit, Oulton Park, Easter 1977. The Americans won the series that year for the second time

Pat
DAMEN
SUZUKI

TEXACO
TEAM SUZUKI

Baker, Steve McClaughlin and Phil McDonald – all were on either Yamaha or Suzuki machinery. A blizzard at Brands Hatch on Easter Friday meant that the first round was snowed off, so the '75 series was run on just two circuits, Mallory and Oulton.

Even though Roberts crashed in the wet at Oulton Park, earlier wins and excellent back-up from the likes of Aldana, Romero and Castro still meant that the Americans gained their first series victory, the final scoreboard reading, 278–248.

Ironically, the Americans were to suffer from lack of star riders when it came round to selecting the 1976 team. Dave Aldana and new AMA champion Gary Scott were both sidelined after Daytona crashes, while Yvon Du Hamel put himself out of the reckoning after taking a tumble whilst racing a snowmobile in his native Canada. Also out of contention were Steve McClaughlin and Don Castro, who couldn't find suitable bikes.

In addition American Yamaha had announced massive cut-backs from road racing, leaving only Kenny Roberts and Steve Baker untouched. The final team consisted of Kenny Roberts, Steve Baker (both on super quick factory Yamaha OW31's), Gary Nixon, Pat Hennen, Gene Romero, Ron Pierce, Pat Evans and Randy Creek . . . strong at the front, weak at the tail end.

Much to the disgust of the Americans the British team was back to its full potential, in fact it was probably the strongest ever with; Read, Potter, Parrish, Grant, Ditchburn, Sheene and John Williams. Dave Croxford on the works Norton Cosworth Challenge was also included, but was soon axed after a poor showing in the first race at Brands Hatch. His replacement Ron Haslam put in some excellent performances to justify his inclusion.

The man of the series however, proved not to be Kenny Roberts, but Steve Baker. The Canadian won four of the six races and finished second and fourth in the remaining two, thereby scoring 92 points, one of the highest ever in the series.

Unfortunately further down the field the American team couldn't match the Brits, the final result running out at 412–384, so the trophy returned to

In 1979 Randy Mamola burst onto the scene, he shown here in action on a Yamaha in that year's Transatlantic series. He went on to become a works GP star for Yamaha and Cagiva amongst others during the 1980s

British hands once more. But there is little doubt that with stars such as Aldana, Du Hamel, Castro and Scott the result could well have been very different.

Towards the end of the 1970s, American Match Race series teams began to sport more and more Grand Prix stars. To start with Kenny Roberts, Steve Baker and Pat Hennen formed the core. Then came a new rank including Mike Baldwin (who outscored everyone in 1979) and Freddie Spencer who made his Transatlantic debut in 1980.

The year 1979 saw the event with new sponsorship injection from Philip Morris after six years of John Player support came to an end. As for results, America won in 1977, 1979 and 1980, with Britain taking the series in 1978.

The year 1980 is a convenient date to close this particular account of Transatlantic Match Race series history. It actually continued until 1983 before being axed, to re-emerge in 1990. But in reality from the beginning of the 1980s it was a mere shadow of its former self – the top stars were not allowed to compete because of clauses in their works contracts. Instead, their efforts were reserved for the ever growing number of Grand Prix races around the world; ensuring the golden era of the Anglo-American Match Races would always be the 1970s.

Teenager Randy Mamola pictured in early 1979. By then the Americans had begun to display their road racing talents to the full, courtesy of the Anglo-American Match Race Series

11
King Kenny

In his early days Kenny Roberts was equally proficient on tarmac or dirt. He is seen here with his twin cylinder 650 cc Yamaha flat tracker in 1973

Kenny Roberts was born in California on the last day of December 1951; he had his first competitive motorcycle race at the tender age of 16. There followed a truly star studded career which saw him go on to win 33 National victories (making him second in the all-time American winners list), 2 AMA Grand National Championships, 3 500 cc World Championships; and after his racing career was over, the position of a world class racing team manager.

But perhaps most important of all, and certainly as far as this particular book is concerned, he was the first American to win the FIM 500 cc road racing Championship title. It is perhaps little wonder then that racing fans in all corners of the world have given him the title of 'King Kenny'.

Kenny's first race came in 1966. Then in 1970 he was signed up by Yamaha-America and the following year saw him race for the initial time in the Expert category.

A decisive point in his career was the year 1972 when the young Roberts came under the wing of the Australian Kel Carruthers, the 1969 250 cc World Champion. Carruthers had settled in San Diego; quite simply he had found that in the early 1970s he could earn during a single season in the States the amount which it had taken him five years to accumulate racing on the European GP scene. With Carruthers as his mentor, Kenny Roberts really went places.

His first AMA National victory came that same year, 1972, when he won the 4th round in the series at Houston, Texas. Roberts ended the season 4th in the AMA championship with 871 points, behind the No 1 plate holder Mark Brelsford, Gary Scott and Gene Romero.

The next year, 1973, Kenny swept everything before him . . . proving himself a winner on both tarmac and dirt. That year Carruthers looked after his road race equipment, whilst the dirt track XS650 four-stroke twin Yamahas were prepared by veteran tuner Shell Thuett.

Kenny's mentor Kel Carruthers the 1969 250 cc World Champion. Kel is pictured after winning the 250 cc race at Daytona in 1971. Behind him is his entrant Don Vesco

Roberts testing a TZ700A four early in 1974

At the season's end the 1973 AMA Grand National score board read: Kenny Roberts 2014 points, Gary Scott 1241 and Gary Nixon 887. This gives a more graphic illustration of just how successful Kenny was on the home circuit during 1973.

If 1973 had been successful then 1974 was phenomenal. Not only did Kenny re-take the AMA No 1 plate (now officially entitled the 'Camel Pro Standings') but he also made his first apperances in Europe at the Easter Anglo American Match races in Britain and the Imola 200 in Italy.

At the former he won three of the six races (for full details see Chapter 10); whilst in Italy the headlines read 'Kenny shocks Imola'. This was in recognition of the tremendous performance he made in this his first ever race in Europe (it was held a week before the Easter Match races). Although Yamaha team mate Giacomo Agostini eventually won both legs, it was Roberts who created the main interest.

In the first 98.24 mile leg the 22 year old Californian shocked the Italian fans and won over the sceptics as he almost casually took the lead and opened up a 12 second advantage over the star-studded field, including multi world champion Agostini. Then a slowish refuelling stop, a misunderstanding about his race position and a lurid 150 mph broadslide let Ago build up a sufficient lead so that the Italian was able to refuel and roar back into the race still in front. Making a comeback

3
1
CHAMPION
GOODYEAR
2
BELL
GOODYEAR

Above
Winner of the big money Ontario meeting in 1975 – with victor's trophy and laurel wreath

Left
Kenny and co before the start of a very wet race at Brands Hatch, 1975 Transatlantic Race Series

Roberts set a lap record of exactly 2 minutes – 95.07 mph closing to within 4 seconds at the finish. The second leg again saw Ago victorious, but only after an evenly matched contest with both Yamaha riders leading the race more than once.

The 1975 season was one of mixed fortunes for the Roberts camp, typified by Daytona, where a burnt out clutch eliminated the American Yamaha team leader in the 200 miler, after he had earlier won the 250 cc race on one of the latest water cooled TZ twins.

In the AMA (Camel Pro) championship series Kenny found he was struggling to gain points on the dirt; quite simply the parallel twin four-stroke Yamaha now had a marked power disadvantage compared to the latest XR750 Harley-Davidsons. In an attempt to compensate a TZ750 road racing engine was slotted into a Champion-built dirt track chassis to provide probably the most powerful dirt iron of all time. The 1975 TZ750 engine pumped out around 100 bph and was a fearsome beast of a machine . . . all that power and only a single disc rear brake to stop!

Kenny rode the TZ750 dirt tracker to victory at the Indianapolis Mile. In the process he wheelied and wheel-spun his way through the field after a poor start to snatch a sensational last-gasp victory from Corky Keener (Harley-Davidson XR750).

The Yamaha wasn't the only multi cylinder 'stroker on the American dirt track scene that year; there was also the Erv Kanemoto tuned Kawasaki triple ridden by the likes of Don Castro and Scott Brelsford. Both the Kawasaki and the Yamaha while being very, very fast were both 'peaky' and suffered exceptionally high tyre wear. At the end of the 1975 season the AMA acted, banning these rocket ships from all but pure road racing events . . . not before time in many observers' view!

Because of the problems of suitable machinery for the non-tarmac events, Kenny Roberts was unable to retain his AMA No 1 plate that year, the title going to the Harley-Davidson teamster Gary Scott, who had finished as runner-up in the previous three seasons.

Kenny during a quiet moment at Daytona in March 1978 – even superstars must eat!

The following year got off to a flying start, Roberts being one of four riders at Daytona with the new 140 bhp OW31 Yamaha (the others were Baker, Cecotto and Kanaya). With electronically speed trapped figures of around 180 mph it was perhaps predictable that all four qualified for the front row of the grid.

In the race all seemed fine until Kanaya pitted with his rear tyre worn down to the canvas. Soon afterwards Roberts came near to disaster on the 45th lap when his rear tyre deflated, but he struggled back to the pits where a new rear cover was fitted. Having lost in excess of five minutes, winning the race was now an impossibility, this honour going to team mate Cecotto, who had ridden the race at a slower tempo than the other three Yamaha stars.

Kenny was to come home third in the 1976 AMA Camel Pro series. All events now carried an equal points value and Roberts no longer had the advantage of gaining extra points from his road race victories. Yamaha built improved cylinder heads for the parallel twin dirt tracker, whilst veteran tuning specialist Tim Witham was engaged to prepare them (Carruthers was still responsible for the road race machines and held the position of Team Manager).

Though considerably improved from the 1975 versions, the XS Yamaha was still no match for the XR Harley-Davidsons which were much improved over earlier years.

Behind the scenes there was pressure from the various factions within the Yamaha organisation to have Kenny race in Europe – not just at meetings such as the Anglo-American Match race series and the Imola 200, but also the World Championships.

His first move was to dip his toe into the water of the newly recognised 750 cc class (the category held World Championship status for three seasons – 1977, '78 and '79) where Kenny contested a few rounds. At Daytona he finished 2nd to Steve Baker and reversed this position when he won at Imola. Although he won five Nationals in 1977 Roberts could only finish 4th in the points chart with Springsteen, Boody and Scott in front.

But if 1977 had been a 'so-so' year, 1978 most certainly was not. At long last Kenny and Kel Carruthers had decided to take a headlong plunge into the European GP scene. This was brought about not only by the various Yamaha bosses around the world, but also by the realisation that without a competitive Yamaha dirt tracker Kenny would never again be in a position to win the AMA Camel Pro title. To begin with Kel Carruthers was far from keen about a return to Europe. However, realising the potential he decided to throw himself into making Kenny's full scale GP debut a success.

For a start the two 'Ks' pooled their respective contract monies, they went to the Goodyear tyre company and got a healthy amount of cash as they did from the Lektron carburettor company and Champion Spark Plugs; putting everything into a new organisation called appropriately the K & K Corporation.

Both the Ks held 49 shares each whilst Ken Clarke of Yamaha America had the remaining two shares because Yamaha wanted someone on their payroll to hold a casting vote if Carruthers and Roberts ever had a fall out (which they didn't).

The K & K team consisted of two 250s, a single 500 four and two of the latest OW31s. The team was greatly helped by the 'signing-on' of two top line internationally known race mechanics, Roger Tilbury and 'Nobby' Clarke; the latter man having begun his career way back in 1960 with fellow Rhodesian Gary Hocking.

The 1978 season got underway at Daytona in a most promising fashion – Kenny winning the '200' at a new record average speed of 108.373 mph, lapping the entire field in the process. Then it was off to Europe for the 'rookie' GP contender. However before crossing the Atlantic there was the little matter of the Venezuelan GP at San Carlos; where Kenny made a winning debut, taking the 250 cc race from the likes of Lavado, Fernandez, Ballington, Lega and Mang – all highly experienced Grand Prix contenders.

Before long it was realised that trying to do three GP classes was just too much effort, so after mid season it was decided to concentrate efforts on the 500 cc class. This was also partly due to a series of tyre problems: Carruthers was to comment later 'Goodyear, unfortunately, were simply not up to it'. Kel also believed that without the tyre troubles Kenny could have won three world titles in that first GP season. As it was he won only one, the blue riband 500 cc – still not bad for a first timer.

The 1978 500 cc Grand Prix contest was staged over a total of eleven rounds; Kenny won in Austria, France, Italy and Britain. His nearest challenger was the 1976 and 1977 champion, Barry Sheene. Their fight went to the final round, at the Nürburgring, where Kenny edged Barry for the title, the pair finishing 3rd and 4th respectively. Fellow American Pat Hennen was also a strong contender until a serious accident mid season in the Isle of Man Senior TT (by then a non-championship event) ended a most promising career.

Another first was the use of large motorhomes, the first time they had been used on the motorcycle GP scene. This level of comfort played an important part in the Roberts championship plan; and it also meant that Kel Carruthers was able to take his family along which was very important to him.

Before the 1979 season had even started Kenny crashed heavily during a test session in Japan, suffering internal injuries and a broken back. But

The 1978 Yamaha Motor Corp team which took on the world and won. Left to right: Kenny, Kel Carruthers, mechanics Trevor Tilbury and Nobby Clark, racing manager Ken Clark

GOODYEAR
CHAMPION
BELL
KENNY
10

although he missed the opening Grand Prix in Venezuela, he made an amazing recovery and was fit enough to be on the start line when the second round took place at the Salzburgring in Austria and won the race outright.

This was to be the first of five Grand Prix victories which resulted in his winning the 500 cc World Championship for the second time. Kenny also contested and won the Sears Point AMA National and F750 World Championship round at Leguna Seca.

In 1980, the Kenny and Kel pairing was elected by Yamaha to run the entire factory team effort. No longer was it a small bunch of enthusiasts as in the past – it now had all the recognition and trappings of a pukka Grand Prix effort.

Yamaha sent a Japanese engineer as a full time employee, and the team colours were changed. They were now contracted to Japan, not America. But as Kel recalled 'Nothing else had really changed, we

Left
Kenny in playful mood with Randy Mamola, 1980

Kenny's Grand Prix team, circa 1980

American fan club at the 1980 Dutch TT. The biggest message is reserved for Mr Roberts. He responded by taking his third 500 cc world title that year

Overleaf
'King Kenny' making his debut with the new disc valve four cylinder Yamaha at the 1981 Austrian GP

agv
GOODYEAR
agv
YAMAHA

GOODYEAR
1

went racing just as we had done before. We were still sorting out our own problems'.

If the 'team' hadn't changed very much the opposition certainly had. For a start Barry Sheene had quit Suzuki to run a privately entered four cylinder Yamaha with sponsorship from the Japanese Akai company. This challenge ended with Sheene suffering an horrific crash during practice at Silverstone.

In fact Kenny's most serious rival in 1980 was the American teenager Randy Mamola, who had finished fourth in the 1979 250 cc championship on a Bimota-Yamaha. Also in contention were: Marco Luccinelli, Franco Uncini and Gianni Rossi. All except Roberts were Suzuki mounted. But this didn't stop Kenny taking his third successive title with wins in Italy, Spain and France. He also scored runner-up spots in Finland and Britain. Although outside the scope of this book he later went on to finish third in the 1981 Championship; fourth in 1982 and second, behind Freddie Spencer in 1983.

In that final Grand Prix season he went out on a winning note, crossing the line ahead of the pack at the San Marino Grand Prix at Imola, the last round of the 1983 season. Appropriately behind him in second and third places were fellow Americans Freddie Spencer and Eddie Lawson. It was almost as if he was handing over the baton, because since 1983 American riders have largely dominated this class of road racing.

But if anyone had expected Kenny Roberts to drop out of the racing world and into a quiet retirement they were to be sorely disappointed. In 1984 he not only resurrected plans for a professional riders' organisation and started talking openly about staging a boycott of Daytona, but stated that he considered that the future of motorcycle road racing in the USA lay with a Formula One class limited to 500 cc – just like 500 cc Grand Prix racing – and the scheduling of at least one World Championship road race in North America. He even pointed out that Leguna Seca would be the ideal venue. And as events were to prove a World Championship meeting at Leguna Seca was soon to become a reality.

Roberts rode a 695 cc Yamaha OW69 in the 1984 Daytona 200 which he duly won; then pulled off his helmet and said he would never race there again (a promise he was to keep). The reason was the 50 mph difference in average speeds between the leaders and the tailenders on a single lap. Weaving in out and around an unending string of back markers had

Daytona 200 winner 1983, with Eddie Lawson (right) and Steve Wise. Kenny bowed out of this American classic with another win the following year

1990 500 cc Marlboro Team Roberts Yamaha; Eddie Lawson, Kenny Roberts and Wayne Rainey. Roberts has successfully made the transition from top rider to top team manager

convinced Kenny that it had become a totally impractical event.

Roberts went into semi-retirement after Daytona. But he reappeared at Leguna Seca later in the year. The chance to see Kenny face Freddie Spencer in what Kenny proclaimed would be his last road race drew a record 83,000 crowd. The expected confrontation never happened, Freddie crashed in practice, breaking his collarbone, an incident which cost him any chance of retaining his World Championship title.

Kenny was his brilliant best anyway, setting a new lap record at 1 minute 6.95 seconds, an average speed of 102.163 mph. He was in a class of his own that day, and men such as Randy Mamola and Mike Baldwin were powerless to stop Mr Roberts winning both legs of the race. 'He's the King; what can I say?' shrugged second placed Mamola later.

Leguna Seca 1984 really was Kenny's last race; thereafter looking after the interests of other riders on the Grand Prix circuit. His Team Roberts has included riders such as Eddie Lawson, Randy Mamola, Wayne Rainey and Jon Kocinski. What else is there to say about a record such as this except 'Long live the King'.

12
Latin Brothers – South America

The first eleven chapters dealt with the North American racing scene; but in several respects their Latin brothers in the Southern hemisphere are no less deserving.

Just consider the following: the first ever international motorcycle race meeting to be held in the Americas was at Sâo Paolo, Brazil in 1954; the first American held FIM sanctioned GP counting towards the world championship series was the 1961 Argentine Grand Prix; the first American rider to win a Grand Prix was the Argentinian Jorge Kissling; the first American rider to become World Champion was Johnny Cecotto from Venezuela; and finally the South Americans have an established (and thriving!) motorcycle industry of their own with companies as far north as Mexico (Carabela) to Argentina (Zanella) in the far south.

There follow five stories concerning motorcycles,

American motorcycle racing was not confined to the northern hemisphere. Here Bill Hidalgo practices on the 1200cc Harley-Davidson with which he later set a new Panama rolling start one-lap record of 23.2 seconds for the 400 metre track in 1952

Emilio Vacacca (500 Gilera Saturno) in action during 1952 at the St Monica circuit in Venezuela, where he set a new lap record for production sports machines at just over 70 mph

riders and events which have played a vital role in creating a widespread enthusiasm for motorcycle racing in that part of the world.

Sâo Paolo International Road Races

Run over the tortuous five-mile Interlagos circuit, the races (held over consecutive weekends in February 1954) formed part of a sporting programme arranged to celebrate the fourth centenary of the founding of the city of Sâo Paulo, Brazil.

From a spectators viewpoint the Interlagos circuit had much to recommend it. Owing to its sinuous configuration, the whole course occupied a small area measuring no more than three quarters-of-a-mile by half-a-mile. This area took the form of a great natural bowl, so that nearly the whole circuit was visible from any given vantage point. The riders had less cause to be enamoured by the circuit, not because of the seemingly endless succession of acute bends, but because of the broken and treacherous nature of the vast majority of the surface. This was swiftly proclaimed by the 'imported' European stars as the worst they had ever raced on; in fact minor spills and retirements through suspension failure accounted for a relatively high proportion of the non-finishers. About one third of the entries were South Americans; of the remainder the Italians naturally enjoyed strong local support.

There was works machinery from Norton, FB Mondial, MV Agusta, Gilera, Moto Guzzi, Montesa and Honda. The latter ridden by Mikio Omura was the first ever apperance in an international event of a Japanese rider on a Japanese machine.

Other countries represented included Belgium, Italy, Germany, England, Ireland, Gibraltar, Southern Rhodesia, Venezuela, Argentina, Columbia, Paraguay, Uraguay, Chile and of course the host nation, Brazil.

In the big classes the Norton works rider Ray Amm dominated the proceedings, his only real competiton coming from Alfredo Milani (Gilera) in the 500 cc race and Enrico Lorenzetti (Moto Guzzi) in the

Above
The Southern Rhodesian Norton works rider Ray Amm crosses the finishing line three-fifths of a second in front of Alfredo Milani (Gilera four) to win the 500 cc at the São Paulo, Brazil road races, 21 February 1954

Below
Start of a 500 cc event of the Buenos Aires Autodrome in the early 1950s. Machinery is a mixed bunch of mainly Gilera Saturnos, Triumph Twins and Manx Nortons

350 cc category. Amm took the poor surface conditions in his stride and was not headed in any of his four races over the two weekends.

Moto Guzzi machines were ridden by over three quarters of the riders in the 250 cc class, with the works rider Lorenzetti doing the winning. Best of the local riders was Carlo Ferreira (obviously of Italian extraction) who claimed a second place in the 250 cc and third in the 500 cc amongst his results. Nello Pagani and FB Mondial won both the 125 cc events, but there was stiff competition from riders on MV Agusta and Montesa machinery.

But although the organisers had done an excellent job of attracting so many riders from around the world, and in the process creating a truly international event, there was to be a sting in the tail. Originally, it had been planned to run a third meeting, but it was cancelled; indeed the second meeting almost failed to take place.

The unfortunate cancellation and other difficulties were due to the actions of the organising body, the *Federacao Paulista de Motociclisimo,* which decided to break all its standing financial commitments (both written and verbal) with the riders. This bombshell burst after the first meeting when it was announced that the financial backing for the races had been considerably reduced. The result was that many competitors received no starting or prize money and were therefore compelled to remain in Sâo Paulo for the second meeting in order to recoup a percentage of their expenses. In view of the foregoing it was not surprising that the second meeting was run in a rather hostile atmosphere.

Argentine Grand Prix

Thanks to several South American countries being represented on the FIM Sporting Committee, Argentina was allowed to stage an FIM sanctioned Grand Prix in the years 1961, 1962 and 1963 – all three meetings counting towards the World Championship series.

The first of these took place on Sunday 15 October 1961 at the Buenos Aires Autodrome which comprised a choice of ten circuits. Two were used for Grand Prix motorcycles – the 250 and 500 cc were run on a 2.4 mile course – while the smaller classes were held over a 1.8 mile circuit. However the actual racing was overshadowed by the Ernst Degner affair.

Degner had been a political refugee since he disappeared from the East German MZ team after the Swedish GP the previous month. Not only this but he also led the 125 cc World Championship series. The final round was the Argentinian Grand Prix; and Degner held a slender two point lead over the Australian Honda rider Tom Phillis.

Without a bike, Degner arranged a ride on one of Dr Joe Ehrlichs EMCs. But the week prior to the Argentinian round, the East German federation withheld permission for Degner to compete and Ehrlich stopped the EMC in transit.

When he reached Buenos Aires Degner was still hopeful that he might be allowed a ride on a borrowed Honda, but he was refused permission to start. Even had he ridden and won, the championship result would have been in doubt until the FIM had investigated the East German federation's embargo and confirmed or overruled it.

As it was, Tom Phillis won the race and took the title – the first five home were all Honda mounted. In fact Honda totally dominated the lightweight classes: Phillis, Takahashi and Redman finishing first, second and third in the 250 cc event.

With no works entries in the 500 cc race (there was no 350 cc class) local riders came into their own. The eldest of the two Kissling brothers, Jorge (the other was Raul) won the senior event on a 496 cc Matchless G50 and in the process became the first ever South American to win a motorcycling Grand Prix. Second was fellow Argentinian Jose Carlos

Salatino (Norton). The first foreign rider home was the Canadian Frank Perris on a Ray Petty tuned Manx Norton.

A year later – 14 October 1962 – some 20,000 spectators flooded into the Buenos Aires Autodrome and Degner once again grabbed the headlines. But this time for all the right reasons. The *Motor Cycling* headline of 17 October 1962 said it all: 'Degner takes the title'. And the race report in this much-respected journal went on to say, 'Only in the last few yards of the year's final World Championship round – last Sunday's Argentinian GP – was the 50 cc World Championship resolved. After a neck-and-neck struggle, Ernst Degner (Suzuki) inched ahead of his great rival Hans-Georg Anscheidt (Kreidler) to snatch second place – and his first world title'.

Other winners were Hugh Anderson (Suzuki) 125 cc; the 46 year old veteran Arthur Wheeler with his immaculate Guzzi special in the 250 cc (a fitting finale to his GP career which lifted him to third place in the 250 cc championship table); and most importantly for this particular book, local man Benedicto Caldarella who won the 500 cc on his Matchless G50. As is related later in this chapter, Caldarella went on to win fame for his exploits with the Gilera marque.

Other South American riders to do well included Jorge Kissling who rode a very fast DKW, sponsored by the local subsidiary of the German company, who beat Suzuki star Mitsuo Itoh for second place behind Anderson in the 125 cc race. Jose Carlos Salatino (Norton) and Juan Gamberini (Matchless) of Chile were second and third respectively in the 500 cc event. In the 250 cc class second place went to the former 500 cc World Champion Umberto Masetti riding an ex works Morini. Masetti had settled in south America after leaving his native Italy in the late 1950s.

In 1963 Mike Hailwood rounded off the year's

Benedicto Caldarella leads Mike Hailwood during their epic 500 cc scrap in the 1964 United States Grand Prix at Daytona

Caldarella (Gilera) leading Remo Venturi (Bianchi) at the Shell Gold Cup meeting, Imola April 1964. The race went to the Argentinian star

magnificent riding by winning the 500 cc class of the Argentine Grand Prix – which was once again the final round of the year's World Championship series.

In a race that was shortened from 40 to 35 laps because of failing light, Mike led from start to finish, with second place going to local ace Jorge Kissling, who took his Norton home 15 seconds ahead of last year's winner Benedicto Caldarella (Matchless) – both over a lap behind Hailwood. Other South American riders in contention included: 50 cc, Raul Kissling (Kreidler) 4th; 125 cc Hector Pochettino (Bultaco) 2nd; 250 cc, Raul Kissling (NSU) 4th.

But the real 'news' concerning the 1963 Argentine GP was the many complaints which were made by the works stars when they returned to Europe after the event. These included, robbery, official evasiveness and hopeless organisation – made by none other than Mike Hailwood, Jim Redman and Alan Shepherd. All three bitterly criticised the meeting. 'It was a shocking shambles' said Shepherd, 'just like a gangster film from start to finish. How they ever acquired World Championship status I'll never know'.

Hailwood was equally critical, 'We had trouble from the moment we landed in the Argentine until we took off again for home' he said. 'There wasn't a semblance of organisation, it was fights and arguments all the way.'

A major complaint voiced by all three riders was that during the first day's practising none of the organisers turned up at the track. Consequently, there were no flag marshals, first aid officials or ambulances and no marshals to control the spectators who wandered over the circuit at will.

Other complaints centred around sand and dust on sections of the longer circuit and the fact that several riders had their clothing rifled while they were out practising, despite the fact that they were using the official changing room. A gold watch, a ring and a considerable sum of cash were stolen from Hailwood, whilst Redman and Shepherd also lost cash. After they had protested, the organisers agreed to make good the losses – but they never did.

Letters of protest streamed into the FIM's headquarters in Switzerland from individual riders and teams alike over the next few weeks. This was probably the reason that no Grand Prix was staged in South America again until the Venezuelan GP at San Carlos in 1977; whilst the Argentine didn't get another chance until 1981, some 18 years after the 1963 debacle.

Benedicto Caldarella (in helmet) and Remo Venturi after their titanic struggle at Imola, April 1964

Benedicto Caldarella

The way he challenged world champion Mike Hailwood in their first ever Gilera–MV encounter, during the 1964 United States Grand Prix, was enough to guarantee Benedicto Caldarella a special place in motorcycling folklore.

The US Grand Prix at Daytona on 2 February was the first of the 1964 world championship road race meetings. Everyone expected the combination of Hailwood and MV to win, with the runner-up spot to be taken by either Phil Read, John Hartle, Mike Duff or Paddy Driver.

Caldarella was riding one of the 1957 Gilera fours brought out of retirement in 1963 and raced that year – largely unsuccessfully – by the Scuderia Duke team. Subsequently one of these bikes had been sent to the Argentine subsidiary of the Gilera factory from which it had been loaned to Caldarella.

As the 500 cc US GP got under way no-one could have guessed what was about to happen. The meeting had been beset by a series of problems culminating in a depressingly small turnout of spectators. But all this was momentarily forgotten as the 500 cc race unwound to the fantastic scene where Mike Hailwood, then the undisputed master of the sport, fought tooth and nail for some 75 miles to overcome the little-known, but inspired Argentinian, Caldarella. Only gearbox trouble on his Gilera finally removed Benedicto from the terrific battle, where for lap after lap of the 3.1 mile circuit, everyone present was treated to the sight of Mike Hailwood unable to better this little, grinning South American, except for a few brief intervals, until traffic conditions enabled Hailwood to jump slightly into the lead.

All this was enough to guarantee Benedicto Caldarella an invitation to ride for Gilera in the ensuing big European races. As it turned out, he didn't make much of a mark in the world championship, but in his comparatively few appearances the young Argentinian displayed sufficient brilliance to justify the tag of 'South America's first motorcycling hero'.

He was a second generation dicer – like Hailwood, Surtees and many more. His father Salvador, one of a family of Sicilian emigrants who arrived in Argentina in the early part of the century, was a medical photographer by trade until his enthusiasm for racing and tuning motorcycles persuaded him to change his job during the 1940s. He later went on to establish a motorcycle sales, repair and tuning centre in Vicente Lopez.

In 1955, when Salvador was the 500 cc champion of Argentina, eldest son Benedicto ventured his first racing appearance at the tender age of 15, on a borrowed 150 cc Gilera. Enforcement of the '18 years minimum' age limit put a stop to any repetition of that antic and he had to wait another three years, until 1958 – the season in which Salvador decided to hang up his leathers – before going racing again, this time on a 500 cc Gilera Saturno single.

Runner-up in the 500 cc Argentinian Championship the following season, Benedicto won it in 1960. Not only this but he also became South American Senior Champion, after a series of winning rides in neighbouring countries – one in a 100-mile (108 lap) race on the most serpentine short circuit in the world, at Valparaiso, Chile.

Switching to a brand new Matchless G50 in 1961, he finished third in the national championship. He went on to win the 1962 500 cc Argentine GP on the very same machine. After another excellent season in 1963, including a third behind Hailwood and Jorge Kissling in the 1963 500 cc Argentine GP, he gained the use of a Gilera four.

This came about in no small measure due to the fact that his father was at that time one of the country's leading Gilera dealers, events which led the Italian company to enter him for the 1964 US GP in which Hailwood found himself one of the toughest opponents he'd ever encountered.

Caldarella's European debut came on the demanding Imola circuit, where he duelled with and finally beat Bianchi star Remo Venturi to win the coveted Shell Gold Cup. (A victory which created as many headlines as the Hailwood battle).

More wins followed in Italian Championship races. He renewed his acquaintance with Hailwood in the Dutch, Belgian and Italian GPs. The Gilera, largely unchanged since 1957 except for new streamlining, was no match for the MV on speed, but Benedicto tried desperately hard to overcome the disadvantage. At Monza, he put the lap record up to 120.73 mph and finished a mere 11 seconds behind the World Champion after more than 120 miles.

Dark, stocky, and of gentle temperament Benedicto was accompanied by his father – and sometimes his mother – wherever he raced. Ultimately this cheerful, but determined rider was defeated, not by any lack of ability, but rather by the Gilera factory, who at the very time he needed their support the most, entered a series of crippling strikes which led to financial chaos. The Caldarella team were forced to return to South America without the elusive Grand Prix win – something which Benedicto's undoubted skill so richly deserved.

Johnny Cecotto

Johnny Cecotto achieved what many considered Benedicto Caldarella capable of – becoming America's first ever world road racing champion.

Johnny Cecotto was born on 25 January 1956 in Caracas, Venezuela. His first competitive races, on Hondas – including a 750 four cylinder model – were

Below
Johnny Cecotto (right) and his mentor Andres Ippolito, Italian GP, Mugello 1976

Overleaf
Cecotto on his way to victory during the 1976 Daytona 200

CHAMPION

agv
JOHNNY

made only after altering his date of birth, being 16 years of age at the time, therefore not old enough to race. By the time he joined the European 'Continental Circus' in 1975, he had become South American champion in both the 350 and 500 cc classes, having totalled more than 50 victories in a mere two seasons.

Cecotto's mentor was Andres Ippolito, the owner of the Venezuelan Yamaha importers Venemotos. In an amazing first season in Europe, Cecotto simply blasted the opposition to take the 350 cc world title with victories in France, Germany, Italy and Finland – becoming the youngest ever world motorcycling champion.

But there were problems. No one could doubt his riding skill, but against this was little or no engineering know-how. He was unable to provide his team with any feedback. Some of his mechanics, including Englishman Vince French, were later to comment that he was limited to demands for them to change the tyres. They were frustrated because none of them seemed to be able to get across to him the fact that he should be able to assist them in solving other problems, where vital seconds could be lost each lap through lack of feedback to the engineer in the pits.

This failure in communication meant that Cecotto was often forced to ride a less than perfect machine, and he was therefore forced into unnecessary risks in a bid to recoup shortfalls in performance. One can only marvel at his riding skill, which compensated for these defects with sheer brilliance. There is no doubt that Cecotto had great talent. But even his great skill could not compensate in the ultra tough world of 500 cc racing to which he transferred in the 1976 season.

However there was little hint of this in his opening race, the Daytona 200 which he won at record speed on an OW31 Yamaha (he had been 3rd in 1975, his debut in the event). Cecotto got off to what many viewed as a highly promising second behind Barry Sheene in the first Grand Prix, the French at Le Mans. However this momentum could not be sustained and mid season, just before the Dutch TT, Cecotto's backer Andres Ippolito withdrew him from the remaining 500 cc GPs, feeling that his young protegé was putting himself too much at risk, and had crashed his machine far too often.

Even so, Yamaha still had the utmost confidence in Johnny Cecotto and he was signed up for the 1977 season for the first time directly from Japan, rather than through the Venezuelan importers. In this deal he was set to earn $600,000 – rumoured to be the richest payout up to that time in motorcycle racing history.

The burning question was, could Cecotto knuckle down and become the complete professional? This not only entailed getting back to his winning ways of 1975, but also having the self-control which meant side-lining the good life, the girls and the fast cars to which he had become accustomed over the past few months.

Cecotto had made his European base in Bologna, Italy. He was summoned, together with the other Yamaha teamsters, to Japan just before Christmas

Johnny Cecotto with adoring fans at the 1977 Venezuelan Grand Prix

Cecotto (centre) with Giacomo Agostini (left) and Phil Read; F750 Dutch TT, Assen 1976. Riders were by then rapidly becoming mobile advertising billboards

1976. The brief was to be fitted out for, and test the very latest four cylinder works 500 cc OW20 and 750 cc OW31 racers.

Much was expected of the South American in the Grand Prix arena, but a heavy crash at only the second round of the 1977 500 cc title chase at the Salzburgring, Austria, effectively put him out of the running for most of the season with injuries which included a badly broken arm. But just to prove his capabilities Cecotto made a brilliant comeback to win the 500 cc Finnish and Czech GPs at the end of the season – in the latter event he also won the 350 cc race for good measure.

In 1978 he only won a single 500 cc GP – the Dutch TT at Assen. Other winners that year were Barry Sheene (2), Wil Hartog (2), Virginio Ferrari (1), Pat Hennen (1) and the new world champ Kenny Roberts (4). It was probably the most fiercely contested title race up to that time. Instead Cecotto came up trumps in the 750 cc World Championship (the second year it had been run), to take his second title.

After this, 1979 and 1980 were very much an anti-climax; his best placings in the championships being a 3rd in the 750 cc category in 1979 and 4th in the 350 cc the following year.

It was then that Cecotto made a successful transition to four wheels finishing runner-up in the European Formula 2 Championship with a BMW March 822 in 1982, followed by a Formula 1 drive in 1983 and later still saloon car racing in various marques including BMW.

Nevertheless, Johnny Cecotto will be remembered as the very first American from either South or North to become a motorcycling world road race champion, with his totally unexpected 350 cc title in 1975.

Zanella

The Argentinian Zanella factory is unique amongst South American motorcycle factories; it is the only one which is wholly owned by South Americans *and* which has built and raced its own road racing bikes. Others, such as the local subsidiaries of companies like DKW, Gilera and Honda have had their stockholders overseas; or like, say the Mexican Carabella concern, have only built roadsters or dirt racers.

The Zanella brothers were of Italian birth hailing from Belluno, just north of Venice. They left their native Italy to settle in Argentina during 1948. That year they formed Zanella HNOS Y CIA, specialising in metallurgy. Then, in 1955, the brothers began to

Zanella advertisement from the mid 1960s for their RK125 'over-the-counter' racer

manufacture accessories and spare parts for the fledgling Argentinian automotive industry.

Two years later, in 1957, the first motorcycles were produced, with 80 per cent of the components imported from Italy and the balance manufactured by Zanella. The following year a licence agreement was signed with the Italian Ceccato company for Zanella to manufacture a 100 cc two-stroke motorcycle.

In 1959 construction of a new production facility began, which was completed by the summer of 1960. March of that year saw the first Zanella motorcycle wholly manufactured in Argentina, and in May the Z-Kart – the first Argentinian kart ever made.

Exports of motorcycles and three-wheeled lightweight trucks began in 1961, the first country to take Zanella products being Paraguay (by 1963 the company was exporting to many other South American countries and perhaps most significant of all to the USA).

With the advent of the first Argentine Grand Prix in 1961 road racing received a tremendous boost in that country and by 1963 Zanella machines had claimed 4th and 5th places in the 125 cc class of their home GP.

Much of the early Zanella racing effort came through the local racing specialist company, Riveli and Kissling. They not only built and raced the SS125 roadster, a single cylinder piston port two stroke, but also prepared versions of the basic road bike for long distance endurance racing – for example a 700 kilometre event held in three stages in the La Pampa region of Argentina. There was also a rotary disc induction 100 cc engine for kart racing.

During 1964 a special racing formula was adopted by the Argentine authorities called the *Standard Free Compound*. To qualify the machine had to come from a type in 'mass production' which in practice meant in excess of 50 units per year. There could be no change to brakes, suspension, carburettor, gearbox or frame. Zanella's answer was a special version of the SS125 roadster but with the cast iron cylinder replaced with an alloy component, a reinforced clutch and a special crankshaft with strengthened connecting rod.

Further news came in 1966 when Zanella marketed batches of 'over-the-counter' racers in 125 and 175 cc engine sizes. These were the RK125 and RK175 (RK standing for Rivelli and Kissling). Essentially the two bikes were virtually identical except for the engine capacity. The smaller unit had a bore and stroke of 51.4 × 59.6 mm which computed to 123.6 cc. Running on a compression ratio of 14:1 it produced 20 bph at 10,500 rpm. Maximum speed was almost 100 mph.

The RK175 retained the same stroke, but with the cylinder bore increased to 60 mm. This gave a capacity of 168.42 cc. The compression ratio was lower at 13:1, with the power bumped up to 24 bhp at 10,000 rpm. Top speed was 105 mph.

Versions of the RK125 and RK175 dominated Argentinian domestic racing for the next two decades; by 1974 they were both watercooled and designated RK4 and RK6 respectively – both power and speeds had increased considerably.

Zanella came to Europe in the early 1980s with a successful 80 cc GP racer. They also exhibit regularly at the bi-annual Milan Show and their basic commuter moped is marketed in Italy by the Cagiva organisation – something of which the Zanella brothers can be proud – as they can be of their racing exploits.

Below
The 1966 Zanella RK125 had a capacity of 123.6 cc (51.4 × 59.6 mm). Running on a compression ratio of 14:1 its single cylinder air-cooled two-stroke engine produced 20 bhp @ 10,500 rpm

Overleaf
A factory rider race testing an RK125 at the Buenos Aires Autodrome 1966. The machine was later converted to watercooling.

Battle of the Twins – Harley style

As a fitting postscript, a final look at the Harley-Davidson V twins in their born-again Battle of the Twins racing incarnation. First introduced at Daytona in 1982, Battle of the Twins is now an established and highly popular feature of racing on both sides of the Atlantic. The main participants are the Harleys and the Italian Ducati marque. The sight and sound of these classic Vees doing battle has to be one of the most irresistible events in modern-day motorcycle sport.

Right
Harleys on the grid, Daytona BOT, 1986

Below
Gene Church piloting a 'factory-backed' XR Harley V-twin, Daytona 1984

Opposite above
British rider Nigel Gaile winning the 883 Harley class at Daytona in 1991.

Opposite below
Team Obsolete rider Dave Roper on his way to victory in the very first Battle of the Twins Daytona race, 1982

2
2

Dave Roper
STAR
METRO
HARLEY-DAVIDSON
71

Index

A

Adams, Ray 46
Agostini, Giacomo 144, 161, 163, 183
Albright, Wally 45
Aldana, Dave 87, 137, 147, 150, 153, 155, 158, 159
Amm, Ray 174
Anglo-American Match Races 6, 65, 68, 146, 150, 151, 158, 159, 161, 163
Alexander, Jimmy 17
Allen, Johnny 110, 111
Altoona Speedway 22, 24
Anderson, Hugh 176
Andres, Brad 20, 21, 38, 40, 41, 43, 54, 103
Andres, Leonard 21, 51
Anscheidt, Hans-Georg 176
Argentine GP 172, 177, 178, 184, 185
Arpajon 21
Ascarte Speedway 4
Ascot Park 86, 93
Assen 183
Auckland 73
Austrian GP 167
Autrey, Scott 83
Axtelm, Walt 46

B

Baja 76, 77, 78, 80
Baldwin, Jack 47
Baldwin, Mike 159, 171
Ballington, Kork 165
Baker, Steve 12, 102, 144, 155, 158, 159, 164
Barstow to Las Vegas Run 78
Bassari, Tommy 45
Battle of the Twins (BOT) 188, 189
Baumann, Art 12, 126, 131, 132, 137, 140, 151, 154
Bay Meadows 18
Beart, Francis 33, 37
Beaumont, Roger 99
Belgian GP 179
Bentley W.O. 17
Big Bear Run 76, 77
Bonneville Salt Flats 74, 107, 108, 110, 111, 112, 114, 116
Boston–New York Run 14
Bradley, Rusty 131
Branch, Jerry 54
Branch, Lou 46
Brands Hatch 60, 146, 147, 150, 151, 152, 153, 154, 155, 158
Brase, Richard 37
Brasher, Everett 53
Brelsford, Mark 4, 65, 67, 68, 69, 73, 86, 106, 160, 163
Brighton Beach dirt track 14
Britton, George 34
Brooklands 18
Brushwood, Peter 13
Bryans, Ralph 131
Buchanan, Duane 53
Buenos Aires Autodrome 174, 175, 176, 185
Burgess, Edwin 4
Burnett, Don 54, 98, 99, 120, 124

C

Caldarella, Benedicto 176, 177, 178
Calderella, Salvador 178
Campanale, Benny 33
Campbell, Sir Malcolm 31, 117
Carlsbad 57
Carr, Cliff 153
Carrutthers, Jan 134
Carrutthers, Kel 130, 131, 134, 137, 160, 161, 164, 165
Carrutthers, Paul 134
Carrutthers, Sharon 134
Cartwright, Robert 30
Castle Rock 93
Castro, Don 133, 137, 147, 150, 155, 158, 159, 163
Catalina 44. 45. 46. 47
Cecotto, Johnny 89, 164, 179, 182
Chandler, Ron 153
Chann, Jimmy 87, 103
Clarke, Ken 164
Clarke, Nobby 164
Clinton, Glen 45, 77
Coates, Rod 11
Collier, Charlie 17
Collier, Harry 17
Collins, Nicholas 13
Columbus 53,93
Cooper, John 151, 153, 155
Cox, Arvin 77
Creek, Randy 158
Croxford, Dave 153, 158
Curtiss, Glenn H. 15, 30
Czech GP 183

D

Davidson, John A. 75
Davies, Jim 24
Daytona 11, 13, 14, 21, 27, 29, 30, 33, 34, 37, 38, 40, 43, 50, 51, 53, 54, 55, 56, 60, 69, 95, 96, 98, 101, 117, 118, 124, 126, 130, 134, 137, 140, 144, 161, 164, 170, 171, 178, 179, 182
Daytona Hilton Hotel 75
Deeley, Trevor 130
Degner, Ernst 175, 176
De Paolo, Peter 24
De Rosier, Jake 14, 17, 18, 20
Deverall, Peter 146
Dickerson, M. 110
Ditchburn, Barry 158
Dixon, Freddie 21
Dodge City 19, 20, 53
Dregri, Michael 13
Driver, Paddy 178
Dudek, Joe 111
Duff, Mike 125, 126, 131, 178
Du Hamel, Yvon 125, 126, 130, 137, 144, 153, 154, 155, 158
Dutch TT 167, 179, 182
Dykgraff, Chet 83, 86, 103

E

Edwards, Tim 37
Ehrlich, Dr Joe 175
Ekins, Bud 46, 47, 77
Ekins, Dave 46
Eklund, Steve 75, 92, 106
Elkhorn 93
Elmore, Buddy 121, 125, 126
Emde, Don 140, 150, 151
Emde, Floyd 37
Emmick, Garry 40
Emmick, Ronald 40
Evans, Pat 158

F

Fernandez, Patrick 165
Ferrari, Virginio 183
Ferreira, Carlo 174
Fulton, Walt Jnr. 125, 137
Faulk, Walt 65
Fernley, John 13
Finnish GP 183
Fisher, Gary 153
Fletcher, Gordon 17
Folse, Pete 31
Ford, Henry 11, 21
France, Bill 37, 40, 117, 121, 144
Franklin, C.B. 18
Free, Rollie 108, 110
French GP 182
French, Vince 182
Fulton, Walt 45

G

Galen, Tom 97
Gamberini, Juan 176
Garon, Luis 98
George, Alex 140
Gibson, John 20, 38, 53
Godfrey, Oliver 18
Godfrey, Tony 96, 98, 99
Goldsmith, Paul 38, 39, 50, 51
Good, Russ 46
Goodman, Benny 44
Goss, Randy 75, 92, 103, 106
Gould, Rod 125, 130, 131, 137
Goulsen, Jack 54
Grant, Mick 153, 158
Grant, Ron 11, 13, 99, 126, 131, 133, 134, 137, 151, 153
Gunter, Al 34, 53
Gustafson, Charles 20

H

Haaby, Dan 125
Hageman, Peter 13
Hailwood, Mike 89, 98, 99, 131, 132, 133, 137, 176, 178
Hammer, Dick 54, 55, 83, 126
Hanson, Bob 124
Hare, Bud 109
Hartle, John 178
Hartog, Wil 183
Haslam, Ron 158
Hastings, T.K. 14
Hayes, Jim 99
Headrick, Larry 87, 103
Hedstrom, Carl Oscar 14, 17, 18, 20
Hendee, George M. 14, 17, 20
Hennen, Chuck 11
Hennen, Pat 11, 155, 158, 159, 165, 183
Herz, Wilhelm 110, 111, 112
Hetzler, Dave 99
Hickmott, Barry 13
Hidalgo, Bill 172
Hill, Bobby 39, 103
Holden, George N. 14
Hood, Jim 47
Houston Show 61
Hurmiston, Lee 20
Hutchins, Dick 45
Hutchinson, Don 39
Hutchinson '100' 147

I

Imola 161, 164, 170
Indianapolis 89
Ippolito, Andres 179, 182
Isle of Man 17, 18, 87, 98, 146, 165
Italian GP 69, 179
Ito, Fumio 47, 99
Itoh, Mitsuo 176

J

Jackson, Doug 13

Jacksonville 31
Jack Pine Enduro 78
Jefferies, Tony 147, 151, 153, 155
Johnson, Bill 111
Johnson, Jimmy 46

K

Kanemoto, Erv 163
Keener, Corky 163
Kelton, Bobby 109
Kissling, Jorge 172, 175, 186, 178
Kissling, Raul 175, 177
Kitano, Moto 98
Klamfoth, Dick 33, 37, 39, 53, 54
Kocheise, Fritz 46
Kocinski, Jon 171
Kretz, Ed 27, 31, 33
Kretz, Ed Jnr. 47
Kucera, R. 110
Kuhn, Del 44

L

La Belle, Ed 146
Laconia 19, 22, 24, 27, 51, 53, 96
Lancefield, Steve 37
Langhorne 27, 53
La Pampa 700 Kilometres Race 185
Lascoutx, Andy 132
Lavado, Carlos 165
Lawson, Eddie 73, 102, 144, 170, 171
Lawwill, Mert 60, 68, 73, 89, 125, 153
Le Bard, Aub 44, 45
Lee Evans, Guy 17
Lee, Troy 53
Lega, Mario 165
Leguna Seca 167, 170
Le Mans 182
Leonard, Joe 11, 40, 43, 51, 53, 75, 87, 89, 103, 121
Leppan, Bob 111, 112
Lincoln 54, 93
Lorenzetti, Enrico 173
Loudon 67
Lowe, Chris 146
Ludlow, F. 110
Luccinelli, Marco 170
Luse, Tex 37
Lydden Hill 4, 60

M

Mallory Park 6, 60, 68, 146, 150, 152, 154, 158
Mamola, Randy 12, 158, 159, 167, 170, 171
Mang, Anton 165
Mann, Dick 25, 43, 54, 55, 68, 83, 89, 97, 99, 103, 124, 126, 131, 133, 134, 137, 140, 147, 150, 151
Marcote, John 146
Markel, Bart 53, 54, 55, 65, 75, 87, 89, 99, 103, 106, 125, 131, 137
Marshall, Jack 17
Martindale, Brian 34
Masetti, Umberto 176
Mathews, Billy 33, 34, 37, 39
Mayes, Mitch 78
Milani, Alfredo 173, 174
Milan Show 185
Milne, Jack 83
Minert, Chuck 45, 46
Mitchell, Don 13
Mojave Desert 76, 77
Mondrick, Gene 77
Monza 69, 179
Moorhouse, Arthur 17
Moran brothers 83
Morgan, William 29, 30
Morley, Don 13
Morris, Philip 159
Mosport 11
Mueller, Louis 14
Mulder, Eddie 93
Murguia, Tony 43, 54
Murray, Boris 112

Mc

McHenry, Pat 14
McClaughlin, Steve 158
McKibben, Jan 112
McLaughlin, Jim 43
McLaughlin, John 46

N

Nelson Lodges 55
New York–Chicago race 14
Nicholas, Jody 131, 151
Nicholls, Nick 13
Nicholson, Nick 45, 46, 146
Nix, Fred 125
Nixon, Gary 69, 83, 99, 106, 125, 126, 131, 133, 137, 140, 147, 150, 151, 153, 154, 158, 161
Nürburgring 165

O

O'Brien, Dick 53, 60, 61, 62, 73, 125
O'Brien, Jack 83
Odom, Jim 131
Olds, Ransom 29
Omura, Mikio 47, 173
Ontario 65, 68, 73, 74, 163
Ormond Beach 15, 29
Otoh, Mitsuo 125
Ottaway, Bill 19
Oulton Park 60, 146, 147, 150, 151, 152, 154, 155, 158

P

Pagani, Nello 175
Palmgren, Chuck 68
Panama 172
Park, Mary 75
Parriott, Buddy 98
Parrish, Steve 158
Parry, Geoff 137
Pasolini, Renzo 68, 69, 74
Payne, Sid 124
Pearce, Ellis 33
Penhall, Bruce 83
Peoria 53, 54, 93
Perris, Frank 176
Petrali, Joe 24, 25
Petty, Ray 24, 25
Phillis, Tom 175
Phillips, Jimmy 38
Phoenix 93
Pickrell, Ray 6, 147, 150, 151, 152, 155
Pierce, Ron 158
Pietri, Roberto 144
Pochettino, Hector 177
Pons, Patrick 144
Pope, Neol 107, 108
Postal, Bill 77
Potter, Dave 152, 158

Q

Quattrocchi, Alli 37

R

Rainey, Wayne 73, 103, 171
Rayborn, Cal 6, 22, 56, 60, 62, 65, 68, 73, 74, 93, 112, 114, 115, 125, 126, 130, 131, 132, 134, 137, 151, 152, 153
Read, Phil 125, 140, 151, 155, 158, 178, 183
Redman, Jim 175, 177
Reiman, Roger 25, 53, 55, 60, 89, 95, 99, 103, 111, 112, 118, 120, 124, 125
Resweber, Carroll 25, 27, 53, 54, 75, 89, 99, 103, 121
Rice, Jim 68, 147, 150
Richards, Dan 94
Riveli & Kissling 184, 184
Robb, Tommy 131, 137
Roberts, Kenny 12, 68, 69, 73, 75, 88, 89, 92, 102, 106, 130, 144, 155, 158, 159, 160, 161, 167, 170, 171, 183
Rockwood, Tom 137
Roeder, George 54, 99, 111, 120, 125
Roeseler, Larry 78
Rogers, Scott 37
Romero, Gene 68, 89, 106, 137, 144, 155, 158, 160
Roper, Dave 189
Rossi, Gianni 170
Ross, Larry 30
Roussea, Kim 75
Rutter, Tony 151

S

Saarinen, Jarno 68, 144
Sacramento 83, 93
Salatino, Jose Carlos 176
Salt Lake City 108, 110
Salzburgring 183
Sandgren, Rob 47
San Carlos 164, 177
San Marino GP 170
San Mateo 53
Saó Paulo 47, 172, 173, 174
Savage, Swede 124
Savannah 27, 31
Schaffer, Harry 124
Schaller, Bus 109
Schwanz, Kevin 73
Scott, Gary 69, 75, 89, 106, 158, 159, 160, 161, 163
Scuria, Frank 146
Seagrave, Sir Harry 31
Sehl, Dave 68, 153
Sheene, Barry 13, 153, 155, 158, 165, 170, 182
Shell Gold Cup 179
Shepherd, Alan 177
Sifton, Tom 51
Silverhorn, Chuck 41
Simpson, Joe 109
Singleton, Dale 144
Skipstead, Bob 77
Smart, Paul 147, 153, 155
Smith, Malcolm 78
Sparks, Robert 27
Spencer, Freddie 73, 102, 106, 140, 144, 159, 170, 171
Sprieglhoff, Johnny 34
Springfield 27, 86, 87
Springsteen, Jay 75, 89, 92, 93, 103, 106, 164
Steele, Orie 24
St. Monica 173
St. Paul 53
Surridge, Vic 17
Surtees, John 89
Swannanoa 110
Swedish GP 175
Syvertson, Hank 53

T

Tait, Percy 147
Takahashi, Kunimitsu 99, 175
Tancrebe, Babe 33
Tanner, Ray 45
Tanner, Sammy 93
Thomas, Jess 146
Thompson, Don 47
Thuett, Shell 160
Thousand Mile Trial 14
Tilbury, Roger 164
Tooth, Philip 13
Tuman, Bill 18, 33, 87, 103
Turnbill, Clark 33
Tuthill, Bill 97
Twigg, Donald 131

U

Uncini, Franco 170
United States GP 98, 99, 176, 178, 179

V

Vacacca, Emilio 173
Valparaiso 178
Venezuelan GP 164, 177, 182

Venturi, Remo 177, 179
Vesco, Don 99, 109, 111, 112, 116, 130, 134, 161
Vintners, Robert 126, 131
Villa, Francesco 43
Villa, Walter 75

W

Walker, Eugene 'Gene' 21
Walker, Richard 13
Watkins, Bud 77
Weil, Lance 4, 60, 61, 99, 146, 147
Weiman, Ray 45
Wells, Billy 17
Wendover 108
Wheat, Charlie 46
Wheeler, Arthur 176
White, Jack 34
White, Kim 13
White, Ralph 54, 124, 132
Williams, John 158
Williams, Peter 125, 151, 152, 153, 154, 155
Winton, Alexander 29
Wise, Steve 170
Witham, Tim 164
Witham, Tom 51
Wixom brothers 60
Wood, John 19
Woolley, Brian 13
Wright, Russell 110

Z

Zanella brothers 83
Zylstra, Pieter 61